The Meditations

of

Khawaja Muinuddin Hasan Chishti

Imploring his blessings and invoking his vision,

this book is dedicated to

*Hazrat Khawaja
Uthman Harooni Chishti*

Spiritual Guide of

Khawaja Muinuddin Hasan Chishti

The Meditations

of

Khawaja Muinuddin Hasan Chishti

Dr Zahurul Hassan Sharib

Published in the UK by Beacon Books and Media Ltd,
60 Farringdon Road, London EC1R3GA
www.beaconbooks.net

Copyright © Sharib Press, 2014

All rights reserved. This book may not be reproduced, scanned, transmitted or
distributed in any printed or electronic form or by any means without the prior
written permission from the copyright owner, except in the case of brief
quotations embodied in critical reviews and other non-commercial uses
permitted by copyright law.

Printed in the UK

First published in December 1994 by Sharib Press
This edition by Beacon Books and Media Ltd November 2014

ISBN 978-0-9926335-2-3

A CIP catalogue record for this book is available from the British Library.

The image on the front cover is taken from a Mughal miniature painting
depicting a meeting of holy men.

Contents

Preface vii

Introduction 1

The Illuminations 5

Purification 47

The Meditations 67

Chronology of Khawaja Muinuddin Hasan Chishti 79

The Message of Khawaja Uthman Harooni 83

Glossary 108

Brief Bibliography 111

Preface

The following pages seek to cover what Hazrat Khawaja Muinuddin Hasan Chishti said on different occasions. Every word that he said is pregnant with celestial fire. He was a friend of the poor, the depressed, the deprived and the destitute. His spirit of humanism sets him apart from the considerations of caste, colour and community.

I hope and I believe and I trust that this book will be useful to all those who are willing and prepared to make their life noble, beautiful and sublime. It is a subjective study, based on the published and unpublished books, discourses, and the *maktubat* (letters) of Khawaja Muinuddin Hasan Chishti. His premier caliph and successor, Khawaja Qutubuddin Bakhtiyar Kaki, wrote the *'Dalil-al-Arafin'* which contains the discourses of his spiritual guide. The book has its own relevance as it belongs to the primary sources.

His meditations give an authoritative insight into the things that really matter. I have classified them into three parts, namely, illumination, purification, and manifestation, indicating the nature of the subject matter. I think that the book is the first attempt in this direction. I hope his meditations will secure for the individual concerned the inner peace and harmony which are sought by man in his bondage.

Like many of my other books this one has been typed by Muhammad Siraj and Gulnar. I cannot conclude this preface without acknowledging the help of Jamiluddin who has made some valuable suggestions which have been incorporated in the text – and who, with the support of his wife Farhana, has published this book.

Last but not least I would like to thank Salim Aran for his help in the preparation. I pray in all humility that Hazrat Khawaja Muinuddin Hasan Chishti may amply reward them and give them wages, not only in money but in spiritual blessings too.

Zahurul Hassan Sharib,
Sharib House, Jhalra, Ajmer,
November 1994.

Introduction

Hazrat Khawaja Muinuddin Hasan Chishti (530-672 AH/1135-1229 AD.) is the most outstanding Sufi saint belonging to the Chishti Order of Indo-Pakistan and Bangladesh. He is the spiritual successor of Hazrat Khawaja Uthman Haruni whom he served with dedicated devotion for more than twenty-two years.

His tours and travels took him to different cities and towns in different countries. As directed by the holy Prophet Muhammad he came to India and settled in Ajmer, where he spent the rest of his life in the service of the people.

He identified himself with the interest and welfare of the people at large. His concern for the downtrodden and the poor and the helpless won for him the coveted title of Gharib Nawaz, which means 'the Patron of the Poor' and by which he has come to be called, addressed and invoked. The teachings and preaching of *Khawaja Gharib* Nawaz, his sermons and sayings, his dialogues and his discussions, serve as guidelines for human happiness. His shrine at Ajmer, in Rajasthan, India, serves as a beacon of light and draws a myriad of people of different regions and religions, and of different castes and creeds. The shrine is the locus of attention and centre of their affection.

Khawaja Muinuddin Hasan Chishti was also an erudite scholar. His book *'Anis-al-Arwah'*, in which he has given the discourses of his spiritual guide and teacher Khawaja Uthman Haruni, has been published, as has his *'Diwan'*, the book of poetical pieces, and his maktubat (letters). His other books, namely *Kashf-al-Asrar, 'Risala Mawjudia', 'Afaq-o-Anfas'* and *'Ganj-al-Asrar'* have not yet been published.

He wrote the *'Ganj-al-Asrar'* at the behest of Khawaja Uthman Haruni. It was written for the guidance of Sultan Shamsuddin Iltutmish (1211-1236 AD). The book is based on Qur'anic injunctions and on the sayings and the teachings of the holy Prophet Muhammad. It also contains an elaboration and an elucidation of the sayings, aphorisms, and the teachings of some of the foremost amongst the Sufi saints.

Khawaja Muinuddin Hasan Chishti writes thus about the circumstances in which the *'Ganj-al-Asrar'* was written: "At last after a considerable time, Hazrat Khawaja Uthman Haruni reached Delhi, by the blessings of Allah, in the month of Dhul-Hijjah in the year of grace 611AH *(April 2nd 1215AD)*. That seeker of truth, Sultan Shamsuddin Iltutmish, eager to pay respects, came to Khawaja Uthman Haruni on the 2nd of Dhul-Hijjah in 611 AH.

Upon meeting him the Sultan exclaimed to his holiness: *'For the sake of Allah, Who has given you life and Who has guided you and Who has taken you out of darkness into light and to the path of truth and righteousness; and Who has taken you towards the higher goal of divine revelation; please be kind enough to acquaint me with the divine mystery and, please, agree to accept me as one of your humble disciples and likewise train me in the mystic way of life. I have come to you with a sincere and receptive heart, full of hope.'*

His holiness, Hazrat Khawaja Uthman Haruni appeared to be much impressed and finding the Sultan to be a genuine seeker of truth and otherwise fit, honoured him by consenting to make him one of his spiritual disciples and bestowed upon him the hallmark of discipleship, the cap.

Hazrat Khawaja Uthman Haruni ordered me to write a book on mysticism based on the Qur'an, the teachings of the holy Prophet Muhammad and the sayings of the outstanding Sufi saints, which would serve as a guide for Sultan Shamsuddin Iltutmish, so that his heart would ever be safe for the love of Allah and would accept nothing but divine love alone. He would thus feel inspired by the book and thereby purify his inner self and by surrendering his self and by being absorbed in the thought of Allah alone, he might attain to higher perfection and acquire more and more spiritual powers.

In compliance with the command of my *pir-o-murshid*, Hazrat Khawaja Uthman Haruni, this humble author began to write this book. I divided the book into twenty-five parts. I named the book *'Ganj-ul-Asrar'*. Having completed the book I thus sent it to Sultan Shemsuddin Iltutmish. For some time he was deeply absorbed in the aforesaid book. It so happened that by the grace of Allah the Sultan, having well digested the book, attained spiritual bliss. He also attained spiritual powers and accordingly became one of the saintly men of Allah".

The writings of Khawaja Muinuddin Hasan Chishti published and unpublished, his treatises, *maktubat* (letters) and his discourses are used as source material for the present book.

*The Meditations
of
Khawaja Muinuddin Hasan Chishti*

Part One

Illuminations

❦ I ❧

The holy Prophet Muhammad once said that Allah, with all the rays of light and manifestation of glory, displayed at first His light. His light is unlimited and without bounds. It has no beginning and no end. Like the light of the sun it envelopes everything.

Afterwards this unfathomed and unlimited light created the light of the holy Prophet Muhammad by its own powers. The two lights, like the light of the sun and the moon are shining in the sky. At first there was one light and then two, but the reality of both lights is one in fact.

Subsequently he created the souls of all living beings from the light of the holy Prophet Muhammad, but he created first the souls of the perfect men.

Allah says thus;

> *"Man is my mystery and the perfect men acquire my gnosis and recognise Me in their hearts. They reach up to Me. Had the perfect men not existed then none in the eighteen thousand worlds would have received My gnosis. By producing the perfect men my object is that there may be recognition and appreciation of the truth, so that people may worship Me and recognise Me. Hence before creating the souls of men, the perfect man, Adam, was created".*

❦ II ❧

Knowledge of the *shariat*, the revealed law, is necessary in order to be constant and firm in the *alam-an-nasut* (the world of humanity). It is imperative that a beginner should be absorbed in the knowledge of the shariat.

Let the people learn reading and writing. They should acquire knowledge first and then take to the path of enlightenment. For a pious believer three things are necessary, namely; knowledge, practice and sincerity. Practice without sincerity, which is meant for show, is polytheism. The heart is the place for the attention of Allah. To acquire knowledge is ordained for every person.

Prayer, fasting, charity, and the pilgrimage constitute the pinnacle of the glory of the perfection of Islam. Those who have external knowledge, but whose actions are not guided by sincerity, forfeit the claim of being a believer. Without sincerity action is of no use.

The knowledge of reality cannot be acquired without the direction of a perfect spiritual guide.

❊ III ❊

In religion there is emphasis on cleanliness. Cleanliness in fact does not depend upon external purity. For the masses and the classes an ablution and a bath are the easiest things to do. Inner cleanliness however implies purity of the heart and soul. It occupies a high place. This does not mean external cleanliness, but it means and implies sincerity in action.

For the gnosis of God the perfection of cleanliness is not enough. What is required is purity of the heart. This inner purity is acquired only when you are really sincere in reforming yourself from within and it frees yourself from inordinate desires, sexuality, greed, lust, avarice, falsehood and other evil things.

You should protect your stomach from doubtful and unlawful food and should be free from anger, anguish, hypocrisy and insincerity. You should wash your back in such a way that there may be no unlawful and doubtful dress and you should wash your limbs in such a way that the eye may be restrained from seeing an unbecoming thing and the hand from touching anything unlawful and the feet from going to an improper place.

❦ IV ❧

When, by constant worship and spiritual practices, the soul overcomes the negative things then good deeds are performed by words and actions. However when the self becomes rebellious by the remembrance of other than Allah, then selfish and satanic actions are performed by words and deeds. So it is imperative that you should keep yourself aloof and take to the articles of faith, the rosary, prayer, and praise, and eat less, sleep less, and mix with the people less, so that you may not be involved in disobedience and arrogance.

❦ V ❧

The gnosis of the world of *nasut* is the shariat, the revealed law. The gnosis of the world of *malakut* is the tariqat the path of purification. The gnosis of the world of *jabarut* is the *haqiqat*, the state of reality. The gnosis of the world of *lahut* is absorption into timeless unicity.

The *alam an-nasut* is the world of humanity. It is the material phenomenal world, perceived through the physical senses. The *alam al-malakut* is the world of sovereignty; it is the invisible, spiritual angelic world, perceived through insight and the spiritual faculties. The *alam al-jabarut* is the world of power. It is the celestial world perceived through entering and partaking of the divine nature. It is also the world of the divine names and qualities. The *alam al-lahut* is the Godhead, not perceived, since the phenomenal is absorbed into the deity.

The gnosis of the world of malakut is acquired by saying *'la ilaha illallah'* 'there is no god but God' in this way that, leaving aside *'la ilaha* ('there is no god) you may reach the reality of *illallah* (but God).

At first you should see the light of *'there is no god but God'* in the curtain of the light of the holy Prophet Muhammad, in this way; that the light of the moon is in the midst of the light of the sun. Secondly you should see the light of the holy Prophet Muhammad in the light of Allah in this way; that the light of the sun is in the midst of the light of the moon. You may see the light of the holy Prophet Muhammad in the light of Allah in this way; that the light of the stars is in the light of the moon.

When passing from 'there is no god but God' you reach Allah. You then reach the coveted station and will become a mumin (a believer). O my dear! Take 'there is no god' as the renunciation of negation and take 'but God' as the affirmation of the gnosis of Allah.

❧ VI ❧

Abu Yazid Tayfur al-Bistami says: for constancy in the world of reality and for inner purification for the world of *jabarut* there is nothing better than the name of the Essence, i.e. Allah.

❧ VII ❧

Towards the close of the ninth century of the hijra, the ulema (religious authorities), the pious, the so-called Sufis without a spiritual guide, instead of being engaged in the acts of devotion and worship, will have been involved in the satisfaction of their own desires. They will be preoccupied with their own self, resulting in inattention along the way and forgetfulness of Allah.

Their wearing the cloak and putting on the turban will point to outer show. Many people will be involved in filling their stomachs. They will be self-serving, seeking self-satisfaction.

Some of the ulema and some pious people will be drawn towards the fascination of the world. They will be dictated to by their own self. They will have no trace or sign of the gnosis of the worship of truth. They will be far from the gnosis of Allah. The real condition of such people will be known to the saints who always worship and remember Allah in seclusion.

❧ VIII ❧

To be united with Allah you should ever be engaged in inner remembrance with all your heart and soul.

IX

The knowledge which contributes and leads to inner illumination is *ilm al-ladunni*, the knowledge received directly from on high, which is the fruit of inspiration. This knowledge is the knowledge of Allah. It is not permissible to disclose its sanctity to everyone. Not everyone has enough strength to hear its secret abounding.

X

Those less courageous and enthusiastic adherents of the shariat - the ulema and the pious - when they hear the secret of God from the perfect and enlightened ones, cast doubt upon it and refuse to believe it. They think it to be impossible. It is imperative then that the gnosis of inner reformation, worship and the training of the world of *jabarut* should not be given to each and everyone. It should be reserved for the sincere seeker in quest of the reality and for the perfect man.

XI

The combination of the gnosis of man concerns the self, the heart and the spirit. The self is the abode of Satan. The heart is the meeting place of the angels and the spirit is the focus of the attention of benevolent God. The quality of the self implies this world, the quality of the heart implies heaven, and the quality of the spirit implies the inner secret.

XII

A believer remembers Allah in his heart all the time. Too much remembrance is always due to keeping the Beloved dear in the heart.

❈ XIII ❉

O, my dear! To remember with the tongue is the knowledge of qaal (hearsay). So long as a sincere seeker does not free himself from his reason and intellect, constancy and absorption are not acquired. So long as you are not engaged and absorbed in replenishing the inner self, you cannot obtain the perfection of the nearness of Allah.

❈ XIV ❉

Sentiments and the intellect are two stations. They don't lead towards Allah. Both the stations are of *qaal*. The world of *nasut* and that of *jabrut* are *qaal*. Love and *ilm al-ladunni* (inspired knowledge) are states. The nearness of Allah is not related to *qaal*.

❈ XV ❉

The treasure of the secret of reality is related to the heart and not to the tongue.

❈ XVI ❉

The heart of a believer is a friend, companion, and counsellor. It is the abode of the secret of the Friend. The pious heart of a believer is the throne of Allah. It is the *Bait ul Aqsa* and the *Bait ul Kaaba*.

❈ XVII ❉

The one who does not enter on the path of God with love will not be accepted nor be allowed admission in the court of Allah.

❦ XVIII ❧

Do not ask anything from the tongue of the heart, but ask from the spiritual guide. This is also *ilm-i-qaal,* that someone may say that he has obtained the khirqat (robe) of a particular Sufi order from a certain saint.

❦ XIX ❧

O my dear! Be a dervish! The wisest among men are those endowed with gnosis and the dervishes.

❦ XX ❧

The seeker who is absorbed and lost in divine meditation is a fit person for company, training, initiation and discipleship. Some Shaykhs know this secret as of vital importance, that the one who has no spiritual guide has no religion.

❦ XXI ❧

In the discourses of Hazrat Al-Ghazzali it is given on the authority of Hazrat Abu Bakr that on the night of the ascension the holy prophet Muhammad saw on all four sides the majesty of Allah and the curtain of light brighter than the light of the sun.

In the night of the ascension, Allah entrusted ninety thousand divine secrets to the holy Prophet Muhammad. He was directed to transfer thirty thousand of them to his *umma* (community), which related to the outer prayer, reflections of the world of *Nasut* and constancy in the *shariat*. Thirty thousand of them related to worship, acts of devotion, the world of *malakut* and to constancy in the *tariqat*. The holy

Prophet was further directed not to disclose the remaining thirty thousand secrets. The knowledge of reality is the treasure of the secret of God. This knowledge should not be asked for from the pious and the ulema. This knowledge is imparted by the murshid (spiritual guide). When the seeker attains to this knowledge Allah then casts His glance of grace and mercy upon him with love.

Allah addressed the holy Prophet Muhammad thus:

'Muhammad! Out of love for Thee I have created the eighteen thousand worlds, but the secret of My favour, the attainment of love and grace, inner guidance and the path of reality are the secrets of My treasure."

Man is My mystery. A perfect man acquires My gnosis and recognizes Me in his heart. I am Myself love and the personality of inner and outward existence is My personality.

Woe to those ulema and the pious in thy umma who do not take me in and do not pay any heed and attention to Me and by inner worship do not recognise Me. They are absorbed in their own personality. They are like brutes and their Islam is allusive and meant for hell.

'O, Muhammad! Whosoever is fond of thee and Me, people become fond of him. O, Muhammad! I am a friend of the one who keeps Me dear in his heart and remembers Me sincerely and does not ever forget Me.'

❦ XXII ❧

The holy Prophet Muhammad is light and the holy Qur'an is also light. The holy Qur'an is of three types. Firstly, there is the Qur'an that has its beginning and end with the writing on paper with ink. This is creation. Reciting it with the tongue is necessary for the ulema, the pious and the masses.

Secondly, there is the type of holy Qur'an that contains within it explanations, praises, narrations, and assertion of the divine message and the names of the God given words. The explanations and the narrations of the God given words do not form part of the creation.

Thirdly, there is that type of holy Qur'an that contains explanations of the divine message and of the secrets of the divine words. The saints and the lovers of Allah, due to ecstasy and being lost in the existence of God, preach gnosis and love with the tongue of the heart. The explanation of the divine words cannot be acquired and understood without the guidance of the murshid. When a sincere seeker, living for a long time in the company of a perfect murshid, attains the perfection of the knowledge of the spiritual states of enlightenment and rapture, associated with passage along the spiritual path, then by the grace of Allah and through the display of supernatural powers, constancy is attained.

❦ XXIII ❧

Once Hazrat Umar asked the holy Prophet Muhammad, "Where is Allah." The holy Prophet replied, "In the heart of the people." Then he inquired about the gnosis of the heart. The holy Prophet replied, "The heart of a *mumin* (believer) is the mirror of Allah. It is between the two fingers of Allah. He keeps an eye on the heart of a *mumin* and a Muslim day and night.

Thereupon Hazrat Umar inquired as to what was the difference between the *mumin* and the Muslim. The holy Prophet explained: "The *mumin* is engaged in silent and concealed remembrance in all sincerity. The heart of a Muslim does not do silent remembrance". In worship and acts of devotion this is the difference. A pious person is a Muslim and an enlightened person is a *mumin.*

One day the holy Prophet said to his companions that God's command had been received to this effect, that to earn His pleasure one should take to generosity. The thing given in His way is the thing that one keeps dear to one's heart.

❦ XXIV ❧

According to those treading the path of civility, the sign of blasphemy leading to perdition is this, that a person may take to worship:

- in order to get salvation
- because of the temptation of heaven
- in order to get the beautiful damsels in heaven
- because of the fear of hell
- because of the agony at the time of death
- because of the fear of being examined by Munkar and Nakir

- because of the consideration of the rendering of the account on the Day of Judgement
- because of the fear of traversing the *pul sirat* (the very narrow bridge over the gulf of hell that leads to heaven).

❦ XXV ❧

Whatever acts of devotion are performed for your own replenishment they are not performed for Allah. Hence such worship is the action of the self.

❦ XXVI ❧

Every mundane worship is paganism. The worship of idols is idolatry, which deviates from the right path.

❦ XXVII ❧

The sincere and enlightened persons regard inner confusion, doubts and diffidence as repugnant idolatry.

❦ XXVIII ❧

The offer of worship with the idea that one may be prominent in the assembly and that people may become one's disciples and be obedient to one is the worship of the self. The simple reason is that there is no element of sincerity in such worship of Allah, hence it is idolatry. Idolatry is the handiwork of Satan. The sincere enlightened ones describe such confusion and inner conflict as a vicious and vile idolatry.

❦ XXIX ❧

The worship that is done for worldly ends, (i.e. the worship which betrays self interest, greed, and lust and seeks pleasure in both the worlds) is an idol in itself. According to those treading the path of enlightenment it is a profanity and not the worship of Allah. By this type of worship you can never attain the nearness of Allah.

❦ XXX ❧

The worship that has the underlying idea that on account of it people will be drawn and offer gifts and presents - such worship does not lead to the nearness of Allah. The sincere enlightened persons call this the idolatry of the rosary.

❦ XXXI ❧

Thoughts coming during worship such as 'where is Allah in the heart?' etc., constitute, according to the enlightened persons, debased idolatry.

❦ XXXII ❧

If, during the ritual prayer the imam leading the prayer, after the first *takbir* (saying *'Allahu Akbar!'*), may prolong or cut short the recitation and in the sunnat part of the prayer, (which are not conducted with the imam) the heart may be diverted towards the holy Prophet Muhammad and in the obligatory part it may drawn towards Allah, the sincere enlightened persons treat it as innocent idolatry.

❈ XXXIII ❊

Illusive or figurative idolatry is when, due to abundant actions and being impelled by the force of habit, you may seek praise, name and fame from the people. In other words when you take mankind without Allah in-between, as the solver of difficulties and expect unasked charity from the people. This is relying on other than Allah and means the reposing of trust in the people. Giving such thoughts and things a place in the heart constitutes idolatry. The sincere seekers call it and treat it as hyperbolic idolatry.

❈ XXXIV ❊

If the intoxicated seeker is engaged in secret prayer in the world of *jabarut* and by mere chance constancy in the station of love is not shown and is thus stopped from proceeding further; or if the heart is engaged in the remembrance of Allah and the soul is diverted from the sweet harmonious voices of the *qawaals* (Sufi troubadours) or from the meaning of the verses sung or recited; the sincere devotees regard these divine doubts as real idolatry. When the intoxicated seeker passes beyond the station of real idolatry, then at that time, he reaches the real pinnacle of being united with Allah.

❈ XXXV ❊

It is imperative and necessary that you have the knowledge of the shariat and know and understand what is lawful and permissible and what is unlawful and prohibited. In other words that you know how to distinguish what is permitted and what is not permitted by the shariat.

❦ XXXVI ❦

If someone is involved in robbery, theft, gambling etc. with the idea that in the last years of his life he will offer repentance and thus will become penitent, such penitence is called optional or voluntary repentance. But sincere or free repentance is to promise to sin no more. It is free from hypocrisy. It implies that, remembering every sin and recalling every mistake of omission and commission, you may be penitent and offer repentance and may make firm determination not to repeat the same thing again.

The one who in his mundane affairs, takes to negligence; the one who, due to an evil intention and diabolic action for the attainment of an objective, takes to falsehood and slander; the one who, forgetting his own sins, finds fault with others and who, treating sin as no sin, offers repentance every day only to sin again and thus remains engaged in evil deeds, impiety and wickedness; the repentance of such a one, who is vacillating and deceptive, is not accepted by Allah.

The gnosis of real repentance is this, that when in silent worship there may arise fear, uncertainty, doubt and diffidence in your heart, you may immediately and solemnly say and recite: 'I ask forgiveness of Allah' or 'Allah forgive me'. But such a course of action is not possible without the training given by the perfect spiritual guide and its elucidation and explanation are not possible without the gnosis of the sentiments of inner reform and replenishment.

❦ XXXVII ❧

The real religion is this, that you should follow the spiritual guide with the utmost sincerity and show him respect, obedience and submission. In inner obedience the spiritual guide is like a path and the guide is Allah.

Religion is marked by sincerity and not by a state of being mixed. Warm attachment is stationary and sincerity is dynamic. The sincerity of the pious is ever engaged in seeking the gnosis of God. O my dear! Figurative religion is the distant voice. Religion is adopted for this purpose that it may enable the seeker to reach the sought. There is no religion better than this, that in the beginning the seeker may renounce his habits for the simple reason that the worship of habit is far from the real religion. When the sincere seeker acquires perfection, then he has nothing to do with anyone except the religion of the Beloved.

If religion may enable you to reach up to God, then it is Islam, but if it does not guide you in this direction then, then it is worse than infidelity or unbelief. The seeker of truth has nothing to do with religion, not the founder of religion, nor with the religion of someone else. The enlightened ones don't know of any religion, except the religion of God.

The spiritual disciple who has no absorption in being himself present and in observing the people and who has not tasted the passing away of the passing away of the self in annihilation, and who is still in the pen of the shariat, is deprived of the union of the Beloved.

Khawaja Junaid was asked by his disciples what was his religion. He replied: 'I follow the religion of God'. Religion is of two kinds. One is the religion of the shariat and the other is the religion of the haqiqat.

❦ XXXVIII ❧

The heart of the believer is the station of *jam'* (gathering*).* *Jam'* in the heart is the pilgrimage of the humble. To acquire real *jam'* in the heart is not possible for everyone. When this real *jam'* is acquired, then due to reading and reciting the Qur'an, due to sincerity of the heart and due to inner obedience, the sincere seeker reaches *jam' al-jam'* (the gathering of gathering). It implies the understanding and appreciation of the manifestation of the qualities of the attributes (of Allah),....that one may take Islam as the manifestation of glory, dignity and power, and that one may follow assiduously the manifestation of the name Hadi (the Guide), keep oneself aloof from vices, error and perdition and save oneself from deviation from the right path.

❦ XXXIX ❧

The majesty of Him is acquired in the eternal and the real majesty is seen then.

❦ XL ❧

O, my dear! That prayer is not divine in which, due to the process of standing and prostrating and bowing, I and Thou remain in between. That prayer is not divine in which outwardly there is worship of Allah but in practice it is carnal or lustful.

❦ XLI ❧

Retirement for Allah's worship is of three kinds, namely retirement of the world of *nasut*, of the world of *malakut*, and of the world of *jabarut*.

❦ XLII ❧

Hazrat Abdullah Ansari says that: 'A sincere seeker, on account of the training imparted to him by the spiritual guide, attains the nearness of Allah within ten years'. According to Shaykh Shibli the sincere seeker attains the nearness of Allah in three years. Hazrat Dhul-Nun of Egypt says that in the third *chilla* (forty days of retirement in a cell or mosque) the sincere seeker attains the nearness of Allah.

❦ XLIII ❧

Al-Ghazzali was asked to define tawhid (unity of God). He explained it thus: '*Tawhid* is to make all One, to see the One, to know the One, and to count the One.

'O, my dear! To think in terms of 'I am' and 'my existence' and that there is also the existence of Allah is being misguided. There are not two existing but there is only One existing and present and this is the existence of Allah. Except the existence of Allah there is no other existence. All that is in the universe is the existence of Allah. So long as you continue to look towards yourself, you will not see Allah. When you do not see yourself in-between, then you will see Allah. Except the One there is no other existing. There are not two existing. Either you may call everyone Allah or you may call all the Essence.

❦ XLIV ❧

Sharaha'i is to follow the interior ulema, the learned people equipped with the principles and practices of Islam which is famous for actions and glorious vision. The religion of *haqiqat* implies obedience and submission to the world of *jabrut*.

❦ XLV ❧

There is the guidance of Allah for those walking in the path of the heart. So their religion is Allah. Khawaja Shibli says: For thirty years I was with Allah, talking to Allah and continued to hear what Allah said. But the people thought that I was with them and talking to them and listening to their talk.' When an enlightened person is freed from seeing and not seeing the Friend, then he secures liberation from all suffering, trials, and troubles.

❦ XLVI ❧

There is no greater or more awful calamity in your own existence than the adherence to habits. There is no poison deadlier than this; that you may desire to enrol spiritual disciples. The traveller in search of the truth who longs to have spiritual disciples does not reach the high station.

❦ XLVII ❧

O, my dear! Leave the trifles and adopt the real religion. The reality of religion is to be immersed in the morals, manners and affability of Allah. The sincere, best and most accomplished religion is the real religion.

❦ XLVIII ❧

With the gnosis of the world of *Jabarut*, there is constancy in the nearness of Allah.

❦ XLIX ❧

The pilgrimage to the outward Kaaba is performed by spending silver and gold, but the pilgrimage to the real Kaaba is performed by spending your heart and life. Nobody can understand the real Kaaba, except the enlightened person and the Sufis.

He is to be pitied who has not performed the pilgrimage in his lifetime. The one who enters the Kaaba of the heart sees Allah. The one who enters the Qibla of the majesty of the real Beloved takes it to be the real Qibla. At that time he enters the recitation for the preservation of the heart. If in this condition, out of his own will or authority, he turns towards the outer Qibla, then he is an infidel.

❦ L ❧

With the spiritually inspired lovers everything is a hindrance to the path except the Beloved.

❦ LI ❧

The heart of those following the *haqiqa*t, when it is tuned and turned towards the real purpose it is called an arch by the enlightened ones. But if you are not employed for Allah, but only want to secure a high social status, then you are behaving impiously.

O, my dear! Try to achieve the sentiments of reforming so that you may get the protection of the world of *jabarut*, and that you may get the real arch.

❈ LII ❈

Travelling is of four kinds. It may be travelling which is good and proper for the time being. It may be contented travelling. It may be customary travelling. It may be real and just travelling.

Travelling which is good and proper for the time being is to go out for your own work and business.

Contented travelling is to undertake travelling for the pleasure of Allah. This type of travelling is undertaken by the *qalanders*, the dervishes, the *faqirs* and the contented.

Customary travelling is that undertaken for the pilgrimage to the Kaaba. But the sincere seekers do not find the smell of the gnosis of Allah therein.

Real travel is not possible without the training and direction of the perfect spiritual guide. It is acquired by following the holy Prophet Muhammad and by living ever in the vigilance of the nearness of Allah.

❈ LIII ❈

Man is born of a father and mother. Among them are some who are mumin (believers), some are Muslims, and some are idolaters. In addition to these there is amongst them a secret group and an apparent group, There is also one (group) who subscribe to evil.

Man is created in four classes or categories. Among them some are engaged in act of devotion and worship of Allah, and there are some engaged in lustful and voluptuous actions. They are engaged in self-worship.

❦ LIV ❧

Woe to those persons who are engaged in negligence, suffering, self-worship, and in the satisfaction of their inordinate desires! O, my dear! Be careful and do not waste life. Allah has created thee for His own remembrance. So be engaged in Allah and throw aside the love of the world.

Those ulema and the pious are indeed wise who do not stay in the world of *nasut* and in the world of *malakut*, but passing through them reach the world of *jabarut*, due to the training of the murshid.

❦ LV ❧

The true lovers of Allah are absorbed in the thought of Allah and live in the protection of the nearness of Allah. The prophets get the nearness of Allah in the station of prophethood and the saints attain the perfection of the station of sainthood. In an invisible world the lover becomes the Beloved. The lover who sees in the mirror of Allah the face of the Beloved, is himself in fact the Beloved, who in his mirror of Allah sees his face, i.e. whatever the lover sees, hears and says, is the real Beloved.

❦ LVI ❧

When an enlightened person dips deep and is encircled, he becomes indifferent to suffering, fear and hardship. Those who are drowned in the ocean - what have they to do with fear, trials and tribulation? There is no past and future there. All is present and in the present they are themselves the time.

❧ LVII ☙

O, my dear! The pinnacle of love is this, that you may see your own personality as the personality of the Beloved. As seeing one candle in a thousand mirrors, a thousand candles are seen, but in fact there is one candle in all the mirrors. Likewise there is the manifestation of one light in the two eyes.

The lover and the Beloved are two names. The station of the lover is *talwin* (change) and the station of the Beloved is majesty, dignity, authority and power. When the lover does not see himself in-between, then his own personality appears to him as that of the Beloved, and when he does not see the personality of the Beloved in-between, then his own personality appears to him as that of the lover. This station is of the utmost unity of love. In this station Mansur said: 'I am the Truth' and Abu Yazid uttered the words: 'Glory to My Majesty!'

So the enlightened one sees himself from himself, talks himself to himself, hears himself from himself, and seeks himself from himself. When a seeker covers the station of "There is none except God" with love, then there remains nothing except the Absolute self. But the one who professes love and may see himself in-between, he is an infidel amongst those treading the path of enlightenment.

Know this that the heart is the window of the path of love, and that it is in-between the two fingers of Allah.

Allah created Adam and showed His manifestation in him. In the existence of Allah there is nothing beside Allah, i.e. in one existence there are not two existing, but there is only one existence and that is the existence of Allah.

❦ LVIII ❦

Shaykh Sa'di sought guidance from Khawaja Khidr who advised him, that to be safe from the suffering and torture of the hereafter he should ever try to seek salvation and forgiveness. You should be engaged with all your heart in the service of and obedience to the Friend, and be ever engaged in worship.

The worldly people believe that there is Allah, and that He is omnipotent and omnipresent, but by such a belief the nearness and the unity of Allah are not achieved. Whatever path the sincere seekers try to adopt, the nearness of Allah cannot be attained without the guidance of the spiritual guide. There is no other way of achieving the nearness of Allah, except by the training and the company of the spiritual guide and being in contact with him.

❦ LIX ❦

Shaykh Dhul-nun al-Misri says for the guidance of the spiritual disciples, that in the initial state of the *alam al-malakut* (the world of sovereignty) he made an invocation: 'O, Allah! Where art Thou? Where to search for Thee?' An invisible voice came: 'I stay in the remembrance in the heart'.

Khawaja Abu Yazid Tayfur al-Bistami says that in the initial stage he made an invocation saying: 'O, Allah! Where is the path? How can I be freed?' A voice came to the effect that: 'Among all the paths, the path of the heart is the best of all'.

Khawaja Shibli says that in the initial stage he made an invocation to the effect: 'O, Allah! Where art Thou in the assembly? Where can I find Thee? 'A voice answered: 'I am in the mental recollection of the pure heart and not in the vocal recollection'.

❧ LX ❧

Shaykh Ahmad al-Ghazzali says that the one who has no spiritual guide has no religion. Whosoever has no religion has no enlightenment. He has no feelings and sentiments in fact. Whosoever has no feelings and sentiments has no love. He has no spiritual guide. 'The saints are under my cloak': a stranger cannot recognise them.

❧ LXI ❧

If a spiritual disciple was blessed by the company of his spiritual guide, but did not get the robe and the cap, then his spiritual discipleship lacked something, for the object of discipleship is the robe and cap of the spiritual guide. and to offer two genuflections as a mark of thanksgiving, so that he may be illumined.

❧ LXII ❧

There are two classes of dervishes. There are some dervishes who, renouncing wealth and position, free themselves from boasting, pride and a superiority complex, and who take to contentment. The second class of dervishes take to submission and obedience after renunciation.

The second class of dervishes consist of those who are fit to sit on the *sajjada* (praying carpet), to accept disciples, to impart spiritual training and to lead and guide others. Even after renunciation this class takes to seclusion and contentment, with the idea that mixing with the people of the world has its own hazards and implies the danger of negligence.

The worldly people come to them and offer them something. Even if it be lawful and permissible, it is not accepted by them. They abstain themselves from the people of the world. They keep themselves aloof. They run away from the people in the same way that people run away from a lion.

⚜ LXIII ⚜

Khawaja Abdullah Ansari is emphatic when he says, that by mere words and deeds you cannot have access to the world of *malakut*, but by tuning the your heart it is possible to have access to the world of *jabarut*.

⚜ LXIV ⚜

The more possessions a dervish has, the more dangers there are to be faced. When there are more dangers there is more struggle and more anxiety. When there is more struggle there is more trouble. When there is more trouble there is more rendering of the account. When there is more accountability, there is more questioning. When there is more questioning, there is more suffering.

For those dependants, money is permissible according to their needs, but not so much as may create dangers. For the seeker who is absorbed and lost some money is necessary for his food, dress and shelter. For if he were to renounce it all then he would be dependent upon others. He would be involved in greed, and greed is the mother of all evil.

The wealthy man, who has discretion and understanding has a great blessing indeed; and the one who has no discretion and understanding is involved in dire circumstances and in disseminating dangers. He becomes far from Allah.

❈ LXIX ❈

Khawaja Shibli writes in his discourses that austerity or abstinence is of two kinds. The first one is real, the second one is metaphorical and implies to eat less, to speak less and to mix less with the people. But the real asceticism is to brighten the mirror of the heart with mental recollection.

❈ LXX ❈

The committing of the holy Qur'an to memory is of two kinds. The one is illusory and the other is real and without meanings (i.e. only the text is committed to memory and not the meanings). To commit the Qur'an to the memory is a figurative and mundane committing. The real committing to memory is by means of the heart.

❈ LXXI ❈

Union is also of two kinds. The one is metaphoric and the other is real. Metaphoric union is this, that with mental remembrance in the world of *jabarut* and *lahut*, the sincere seeker being engaged in the protection of his heart with all his life and soul, may get intoxication. When perfection is obtained in metaphorical union, then real union is achieved. Real union is this, that the sincere seeker, renouncing self-worship, pride, self-conceit, vanity and his self, - may reach the station of union, conjunction, and contact with Allah.

⚜ LXXII ⚜

So long as a seeker continues to see himself, he will not see Allah. When the seeker does not see himself in-between, then the pinnacle of the perfection of unity with Allah will be achieved.

⚜ LXXIII ⚜

The one who does not find Hazrat Ali Murtada present in the real union with all his heart and soul, will be away from Allah: he will not attain the constancy of the station of perfection, for all the ninety-nine thousand divine and mysterious words of wisdom which Allah in the night of ascension imparted to the holy Prophet Muhammad, all of them were preached to Hazrat Ali.

Hazrat Ali was unique and excelled all in the following of the holy Prophet. Any sincere seekers, barring a very few, who do not follow Hazrat Ali and do not establish and maintain a real bond and link with him in all sincerity, and with heart and soul, will remain deprived of even the smell of the gnosis of Allah, in spite of his being engaged a thousand times in acts of devotion, worship, and ascetic practices.

❦ LXXIV ❧

Sultan Ibrahim bin Adhem disclosed the fact that he was engaged for years in acts of devotion, worship, ascetic practices and rigorous spiritual exercises, and that he wasted his life in the company of the learned, the pious, and the devotees. He got nothing. He could not even get the smell of the gnosis of Allah. But when he reached Khawaja Fudayl bin Ayad, he got what he wanted. What he got in his company was the pinnacle of his achievement.

❦ LXXV ❧

It is given in the discourses of Ahmad Al-Ghazzali that sultan Mahmud Ghaznavi passed twelve years in the company of the perfect spiritual guide and teacher, the intoxicated seeker, Hazrat Shaykh Said Ullah of Kerman.

❦ LXXVI ❧

It is said that Shaykh Fariduddin Attar, being blessed by the company of Sana Ullah, attained the perfection of the union with Allah.

❦ LXXVII ❧

It so happened one day that Hazrat Umar, being in the state of the intoxication of love and in the state of being fascinated and absorbed, caught hold of the shirt of the holy Prophet Muhammad.

❈ LXXVIII ❈

It is not good to disclose the intoxication of love to the common people. Sahw (sobriety) is this, that despite being ever engaged in the remembrance of Allah, whatever you may hear, you may distinguish it and know it.

When the lover is overwhelmed by the love of the Friend to such an extent that he may not be mindful or aware of his existence, then his station is called the world of wonder, amazement and absorption.

❈ LXXIX ❈

In the station of *zulf* (the curling lock of hair) and *zulfayn*, the charm of the Beloved and the beauty of Allah's manifestation are in the heart. The implication of *zulfayn* is that it points to the attraction of Allah's grace and to the mystery that conceals the divine essence. The desire to reform within is in the heart of the believer, but without the training of the spiritual guide it cannot be appreciated and understood.

❈ LXXX ❈

The real rosary is this, that you may be attached to Allah day and night. The figurative rosary is this, that you may be attached to the world and the people of the world. If you are attached to them in worship then it is debased and sordid idolatry.

❈ LXXXI ❈

The real wine in a clear heart is the sign and symbol of moving about in Allah, and refers to the virtues and qualities, and to the way of life to be moulded according to the attributes of Allah.

The pure and purifying wine is this, that the divine grace may descend upon the heart of the faithful witness of the truth.

The real tavern is in the heart. But without the guidance of the perfect spiritual guide the absorbed traveller on the way cannot understand it.

❦ LXXXII ❧

The tavern means and implies that in the gambling house of love you may lose your wealth, position, garden, land, and whatever is destined in the universe and in both the worlds.

❦ LXXXIII ❧

The implication of 'the temple and the place of idol worship' is wide enough to cover even the slightest thought of both the worlds occupying you heart.

❦ LXXXIV ❧

Idol worship is this, that the pilgrims on the way may treat pride and fame as the mark of perfection and the pinnacle of glory.

❦ LXXXV ❧

The seeker who thinks himself to be in authority, power, majesty and dignity is an idol worshiper.

❦ LXXXVI ❧

The renowned and unbecoming worship is this, that in seeking fame, a position, a good name, and a good reputation you may be engaged in vanity, show, self-praise and self-worship.

❦ LXXXVII ❧

In the world of jabarut (the world of power) when the intoxication of love descends upon the heart of the pilgrim on the way, and when he, being overcome by the intensity of the fondness of love, stands up and begins to dance in the *sama'* (spiritual concert), then there can be no objection to it.

❦ LXXXVIII ❧

Though the lover hears only the sweet voice of the singer and understands it, yet in the world of *nasu*t this is unlawful, prohibited and forbidden from the point of view of *saluki* (treading on the Sufi path). It is odious and abhorred in the world of *malakut*, (the world of sovereignty).

❦ LXXXIX ❧

According to some travellers on the Sufi path, the *sama'* (spiritual concert) is lawful and admissible, having legitimate sanction. According to others it is impermissible and disallowed.

Although gnosis finds its way in the heart of the sincere *salik*, when the traveller, due to adherence to the world of *nasut* and to the world of *malakut*, stands in the *sama'* and begins to dance then this is not permissible unless he has constancy in the world of *jabarut* and the world of *lahut*.

In the *'Quwwat al-Qulub'*, written by Hazrat Khawaja Uthman Haruni, it is given that the music from the tongue of vision is a type of worship in which Allah has confided many secrets. As in every man there is a secret, as in every face there is death, as in every suffering there is relief, and as in every thread there is work, likewise in every musical instrument there is a melody.

Sama' is of two kinds: *hagim* (affecting violently and rapidly, acting with sudden energy) and *ghair hagim* (which does not affect suddenly and violently but only after one's attention and understanding is drawn to it).

A Sufi should ascribe all the loss received due to change to himself, and whatever perfection of the meaning of reality he receives he should ascribe to the Majesty and Grace of Allah. Time, place, and the company of like minded people are the three strings attached to *sama'*.

By time is meant that the heart may not be lead in another direction (i.e. there may be no thought or desire for a bath or food etc). By 'place' is meant that the *sama'* should not be in an unpleasant dark, dirty or dingy thoroughfare. It should not be the house of some tyrant or someone not following faithfully the precepts of Islam. By 'company' it is meant that there should be sincere and righteous people forming a community of interest.

Those participating in *sama'* should be the disciple of one spiritual guide or the devotees of some family, or dervishes having a common outlook, common ideas and common ideals. For the Sufis having identity of interest, or the *qalanders*, etc.

Proud people, women and children should not be allowed to be in the *sama'*. For people engrossed in negligence *sama'* is unlawful. For those attending *sama'* it is not permissible to talk during the music concert. Those participating in the *sama'* should not shake their heads nor do anything out of their own will. They should wait for the grace of Allah to descend upon their heart.

If somebody, being overcome by ecstasy, stands up, then the other people participating should also stand. If the turban of someone falls off then it should be picked up and placed back on his head. They should look after him.

According to Dhul-nun al-Misri the *sama'* directs the heart towards Allah and leads to the search for Allah.

If you hear the *sama'* for Allah, you get a way towards Allah, but if you hear it for your own inordinate desires, then you invite depredation and misery. In the *sama'* you are united with Allah. If you hear it for the sake of Allah then you will come close to Allah. Outwardly the *sama'* is perfidy, but inwardly it is a warning. The *sama'* of this type is lawful. But the *sama'* which is not for Allah is a disturbing mischief.

Some say that the *sama'* is a source of presence and that a complete and abundant love is obtained from it; so much so that the lover is united with the Beloved. But it is a defect of love. The fact is this, that by the *sama'* two-fold union is achieved, for it gives a place to sincere love in the heart and confers observation on the head, union to the soul, service to the body, vision to the eye, and the voice of the Friend to the ear.

The *sama'* is of two kinds. One is through the intermediary and the other is without an intermediary. When it is heard through a singer it is concealed, latent and invisible, but when it is heard from Allah it is presence. The *sama'* is like the sun from which anything is obtained according to the degree of fondness. No one is deprived. The *sama'* leads to Allah but its constituents are buffoonery. They are a jest, a joke, and they are ludicrous. A beginner is not competent to hear *(sama')* the traditions of the holy Prophet.

Hazrat Junayd of Baghdad says: 'I saw a dervish who came, sat in the *sama'* and died. This is the real sama'. If clothes are given to the singer it is permissible for the dress of the murdered belongs to the murderer. If the dress is not given to the singer, then it is against the precepts of the *tariqat*. Some say that the clothes should be given to the singer with the consent of the imam. Hence, without the order of the spiritual guide the clothes should not be given to the singer.

In the *sama'* it is not permissible to tear the clothes, to complain, to shout, to wail and bemoan, to weep, to knock, to walk, to talk, to drink water, to point to the defect of the singer and to look towards anyone. But when someone hearing the *sama'* is overpowered and the curtains are removed from in-between, and he becomes unmindful, helpless, and unable to control himself, then it is permissible for the people participating to in the *sama'* to follow him in tearing their own clothes.

Sama' should be made a habit.

❈ XC ❧

Our Shuyukh, belonging to the Chishti order have adopted fifteen stations, and have treated them as their modus operandi, their rule and their regulation, their manual and code.

- The first station is of the penitents, which points towards Prophet Adam.

- The second is of the pious, the station of Enoch.

- The third is of the virtuous, which points to Prophet Moses.

- The fourth is of the patient, which pertains to Prophet Job.

- The fifth is of the satisfied, which points to Prophet Jesus.

- The sixth is of the contented, which points to Prophet Jacob.

- The seventh is of the ascetics, which refers to Prophet Jonah.

- The eighth is of thoughtful, the uneasy, and the perplexed which pertains to Prophet Joseph.

- The ninth is of the defeated and routed which points to Prophet Jethro.

- The tenth station is of the instructors and the spiritual teachers, which refers to Prophet Seth.

- The eleventh is of the virtuous and the righteous, which points to Prophet Noah.

- The twelfth is of the sincere, which points to Prophet David.
- The thirteenth is of the enlightened ones, which refers to Prophet Khidr.
- The fourteenth station is of the grateful, which points to Prophet Abraham.
- The fifteenth station is of the lovers which, refers to Prophet Muhammad. If the dervish by the guidance of his spiritual guide is not aware of the stations, then he is still a beginner; indeed.

❦ XCI ❧

It is said that Khawaja Hasan al-Basri, Khawaja Ma'ruf al-Kharki, Sultan Ibrahim bin Adhem and Khawaja Shaqiq of Balkh appeared in a dream, discussing among themselves the true nature of sincerity.

Khawaja Hasan al-Basri said that he is not sincere in his claim of love who does not show patience upon receiving suffering from Allah.

Khawaja Ma'ruf al-Kharki did not agree with what Khawaja Hasan al-Basri said, as this opinion was based on egoism vanity and conceit. According to him, he is not sincere in the claim of love who, on receiving grace, does not derive ecstasy from it.

Khawaja Shaqiq of Balkh expressed his opinion thus: 'In the claim of love he is not sincere who does not offer thanks on receiving hurt and suffering from the Friend'.

Sultan Ibrahim bin Adhem then said: 'In the friendship of Allah he is not sincere who, being absorbed in the vision of the Friend does not forget the hurt'. As, when seeing the Prophet Joseph, the women of Egypt were not aware of the injury to their hands, likewise a sincere lover should be absorbed in the vision of the Friend.

❈ XCII ❦

There are fourteen famous branches of knowledge for the realisation of Allah in this world.

- There is the knowledge of the *shariat* which constitutes a commentary on the divine words.
- *Fiqh* which is the knowledge of religion and law, Islamic jurisprudence.
- The most excellent philosophy which relates to the meaning and appreciation of poetry.
- *Ilm-i-hikmat* which can be found in the books written by the wise and learned. It refers to wisdom and knowledge.
- There is the knowledge of certainty which is to know the intrinsic quality of the names.
- The knowledge of documents and manumissions.
- The knowledge of astronomy, relating to the stars and planets.
- The knowledge of logic relating to syllogisms.
- The knowledge of music which is one of the branches of knowledge.

- The knowledge of medicine which relates to curing the human body. The knowledge of tawhid, the unity of Allah.

- The knowledge of the tariqat, i.e. the gnosis of the world of malakut.

- The knowledge of the haqiqat - the gnosis of the world of jabarut.

- Lastly comes ilm al-ladunni, in other words the inspired knowledge. It comes direct from on high and is the fruit of inspiration.

❦ XCIII ❧

One day Abdullah Ansari asked Allah: 'O, Allah! What is the first work and what is its end. (i.e. what is its reward)? A voice came to the effect: 'First is the work of *Fana* (extinction) and its end is *Wafa* (fidelity and allegiance), while its reward is *Baqa* (immortality)'.

Then he inquired: 'What is *fana*? What is *wafa*? What is *baqa*? A voice then informed him that: '*Fana* is to get rid of the self and self-worship and implies the obliteration of one's own existence. *Wafa* is to be true and loyal to the Friend with all your heart and soul and under all conditions and circumstances. *Baqa* is to engage the heart in the reality come what may.

Then he inquired about '*uqubat*' (punishment*), ma'siyat* (sin), and *kifayat* (being sufficient). The voice answered thus: 'To forget your own sins is *uqubat* (to forget your own sins is a punishment because you do not offer repentance, as you have forgotten you sins). *Ma'siyat* is this, that you may have the patience to offer the repentance which is irrevocable. *Kifayat* is this, that you may be satisfied and content with the remembrance of Allah. To receive blessings and favour without offering thanks in this world will lead to arrogance and pride, impatience in both the worlds is a calamity. Worship without sincerity is to waste your life.

Then he submitted:

> *'O, Allah! Thy grace is eternal. The sin of the self is a stranger. The self is idolatry and the approbation of the people is a rosary. Any misfortune coming from the Friend is a gift and to complain of the gift from the Friend is a mistake."*
>
> *O, Allah! It is indeed unfair that I may ask Thee. Give me salvation, so that Thou art no longer under any obligation and I shall have no requests to Thee anymore.*
>
> *O, Allah! Thou art omnipresent and omnipotent. Thou seest everything. Thou knowest everything. So there is no need to tell anything to Thee.*
>
> *O, Allah! Is this not thy great blessing and grace which thou hast conferred upon the lovers, that they acquire Thy gnosis by means of the training of the spiritual guide and are blessed by the perfection of Thy nearness?*
>
> *O, Allah! If I am a friend then remove the curtain from in-between, and if I am a guest then treat the guest kindly in a befitting manner.'*

❦ XCIV ❧

It is given in the discourses of Khawaja Shibli that the holy Prophet was given by Allah the *khirqat* (robe), the cap and the bowl, in the night of ascension (*Miraj*). He was directed to ask of his companions what they would do if they were given the holy relics. The one who gave the correct answer would get them. The perfect man who was destined to get the holy relics would receive them.

Some time after his return from the ascension the holy Prophet asked Hazrat Abu Bakr: 'O, Abu Bakr! If I give the robe of the caliphate of Allah, the cap and the bowl, what would you do then? Hazrat Abu Bakr submitted thus: ' I will take to more acts of devotion, worship and piety and adhere to you in the inward and outward prayers'.

The holy Prophet subsequently put the question to Hazrat Umar. He replied: 'For the pleasure of Allah I shall adopt justice and give what is due to the rightful claimants'.

Next the holy prophet asked the same question to Hazrat Uthman, who replied thus: 'O, messenger of Allah! For the pleasure of Allah I shall give generously to the poor and the needy'.

Last of all, the holy Prophet asked Hazrat Ali, 'O, Ali! Tell me what will you do if I give you the robe of the caliphate'. Hazrat Ali submitted thus, 'O, messenger of Allah! I shall conceal the faults of the people and hide their sins'. On hearing this the holy Prophet said, 'Allah has so ordered me that whomsoever among my companions may give this reply, I should give him the robe of the caliphate, the cap, and the bowl.'

The Meditations
of
Khawaja Muinuddin Hasan Chishti

Part Two

Purification

❖ I ❖

Namaz (ritual prayer) is of two kinds. The first is the prayer of the ulema, the jurists, and the pious, which is confined to precept and practice. This does not secure the union with Allah. Its reach is only up to the *malakuti* world of the self. The second type of prayer is that of the prophets, the saints and the caliphs, which is performed with a receptive heart. Its reward is the union with Allah and its reach is up to the divine world of *jabarut*.

❖ II ❖

The real fast is to have no spiritual and mundane desires, which means and implies to have no desire for paradise, wealth or worldly positions and power. To think about other than Allah and to desire paradise are the things which break the fast.

The holy Prophet Muhammad has said that: 'Except Allah, nothing is desired to be seen.' He has also said: 'The beginning of the real fast is the sight of Allah, and its end also will be the sight of Allah'. In other words the beginning of the fast is the gnosis of Allah, and the breaking of the fast, its end, is the sight of Allah on the Day of Judgement.

According to the holy Prophet Muhammad there are two occasions of joy for the person keeping the fast. One occasion of joy is at the time of breaking the fast and the other is at the time of seeing the glorious vision of Allah.

The fast of the masses presupposes first abstinence, and second the breaking of the fast at the end. The position of the real fast is different. The real fast on the contrary presupposes the breaking in the beginning and the fasting afterwards. The real fast does not entail any condition for breaking it, but for breaking the ordinary fast abstinence first is necessary.

The people who keep the fast abstain from eating and drinking, but this is not the real fast. It is an unreal fast in fact. In such a fast things other than Allah are not renounced. The idea of the self continues to dominate. Such a fast is useful in so far as that a person may realise the pangs of hunger and thirst of other people and may extend help and sympathy to the sufferers.

❖ III ❖

The *shariat* makes it obligatory to pay five hundred out of every two hundred dinars as *zaka*t (charity). But those belonging to *the tariqat* lay down that out of two hundred dinars only five should be kept and the remainder given in charity.

Zakat is obligatory for the free man. The slaves are exempted. As long as you are not free from the worship and the dictates of your own self, then you are not amongst the free men. Whilst you are not free, *zakat* is not obligatory for you. When you are given to the adoration of your own self, then you should first free yourself from the bondage thereof, so that you may be able to pay the real *zakat*. *Zakat* is obligatory on a person of sound mind and on one who has attained the age of majority. It is not obligatory for a person of unsound mind or for a minor. According to the enlightened persons, the one who is engrossed in negligence and is devoted to the self, is not a person of sound mind nor an adult. It is necessary that you should first free yourself from the bondage of the self, so that you may be able to pay the real *zakat*.

❈ IV ❈

The real treasure is the secret of Allah. The hearts of the enlightened ones are His treasure. The enlightened must give the *zakat* of the secret of Allah from their own treasure to the waylaid and the ignorant.

❈ V ❈

The heart of a human being is the *Ka'aba*. The holy Prophet Muhammad has said: 'The heart of man is the abode of Allah.' At another time he has said: 'The heart of man is the throne of Allah.'

The existence of man is akin to four walls. If the curtain of doubt, diffidence and non-Godly objects is removed, then in the courtyard of the heart the vision of Allah, the Almighty, will be seen. This is the real pilgrimage to *Ka'aba*.

The meaning of the real pilgrimage is that you may so efface yourself that outwardly and inwardly you become virtuous and the heart imbibes the attributes of Allah, the Almighty.

❈ VI ❈

There are four groups of people:

The first group is that of the masses. They are known as practicing the outward rituals. They follow the path of the *shariat*. They tread the first of the four steps of the love of

Allah. Their death in this condition will be tantamount to dying in the pursuit of outward things.

The second group is that of the advanced masses. This group is inclined towards spiritualism, but since those belonging to this group are not acquainted with the inner mysteries, they are sometimes seekers of the world and at other times of the world-hereafter. Their inner eyes are not completely lit by the inner light. This group follows the *tariqat*.

The third group is that of the classes. They are called the people pursuing the reality.

The fourth group is of the selected few, who are called the enlightened ones.

❦ VII ❦

The prophets are like the physicians who suggest medicines for different types of sick person according to their ailment. Likewise the prophets also give medicine according to the spiritual capacity and inner ailments. They give the gift of gnosis so that the spiritually invalided person, recovering completely, may become an enlightened one.

❦ VIII ❦

All the things of the world are His mirror. In fact all are the same, but the ways of showing them are different, as the meaning may be the same but it is explained through the medium of different words. So there is the One and the One only, but His manifestations are different. There can be no doubt that 'Allah circumscribes everything'.

Man however occupies a preeminent position in creation. Man is the image of Allah. There is a distinction between man and man. Some are given precedence over others.

IX

Allah at first manifested Himself in Himself and separating one light from His own light, showed Himself in Himself and showed Himself His glory. They were the Lover, Love, and the Beloved.

X

When Allah separated the circle of the light of Muhammad, all the universe was there in this circle with all the qualities. Afterwards Allah made this circle of the light of Muhammad into a star and looked towards it with love for eighty thousand years and with majesty for seventy thousand years.

From this light He created fire, and from fire he created the wind, from the wind He created water and from water he made dust....subsequently he created Adam from the four elements. When the shape was complete then He gathered together all the four elements.

At first the light stayed in the head, then fire in the eyes, the wind in the naval, and water beneath the tongue. The dust came to stay on the right side....whatever is in the universe all that was produced in man. As there are four seasons in the creation of the world likewise [in man] childhood is the winter, youth is the spring, the time spent in a passive way is summer and old age is the autumn.

The tongue takes water from the heart which is sweet. The nose takes water from the lung, which is sour, and the eye takes water from the liver which is acrid.

Wisdom is in the mind; bashfulness is in the eye; understanding is in the ear; knowledge is in the chest, and love is in the heart. Allah created the four elements. At first He created fire, then wind, after that He created water and last the dust.

❖ XI ❖

For those treading the [Sufi] path first is the *shariat*, Then comes *tariqat*. After that there is the station of *ma'rifat* (gnosis). Last comes the station of *haqiqat*. Reaching this station whatever is asked for is given.

❖ XII ❖

The saints and the sheikhs will be placed in such a condition, that there will be a *Gudri* (a patched garment) on their shoulders. In every such *gudri* there will be innumerable threads. Seeing this their disciples, followers and devotees will hang themselves in those threads and will hold fast to each and every thread.

The blessings of the *gudri* will enable the disciples and the devotees, in spite of the horrors and afflictions of the Day of Judgement, to enter paradise safely; having thus covered a distance which would normally have been traversed in thirty thousand years. They will not face any hardship there.

❦ XIII ❧

The first thing that came to be compulsory for human beings is gnosis. (The *jinns* and the human beings have been created for worship).

❦ XIV ❧

There was a God-illumined dervish who used to distribute whatever he got amongst the dervishes. He used to live in his hut and let no one go deprived. It so happened once that two dervishes, who had attained perfection, came to him and asked for water. The dervish went into his hut and came out with two loaves of barley bread and a cup of water. The two visiting dervishes were hungry. They took the bread and drank the water.

Afterwards the two dervishes looked at each other. One said to the other, 'This dervish has done his part well indeed. Now we should do something for him. Let us give him this world.' The other dervish replied 'If he is given this world he will indulge in sin'. The first dervish then remarked, 'The dervishes are generous by disposition. He is given this world to earn the world hereafter.' They prayed for their host and left. The dervish who had entertained them achieved such a high spiritual position, that he used to distribute a large quantity of food daily to the indigent and the poor.

❦ XV ❧

The one who attains the gnosis of Allah, the Almighty, does not go about saying 'Allah!, Allah!' The one who does so has not in fact attained gnosis. It has been said that: 'The one who has attained the gnosis of his Creator and Cherisher becomes dumb and lame'. The condition of the perfect enlightened one exceeds the station of remembrance, because remembrance is also a kind of separation and according to the enlightened ones separation is a defect. It is given in the holy Qur'an: 'Wherever you are Allah is with you'.

XVI

The people recite: 'There is no god but God and Muhammad is the messenger of God', but they don't know what is meant by non-existence and existence, who is denied and Who is affirmed. This article of faith implies that, except Allah, the One and Supreme, there is none existing and that the holy Prophet Muhammad is the manifestation of Allah.

Hence the seeker should not allow the thought of anyone else and should know the One, the Absolute, to be present everywhere. It is given in the Qur'an that: 'Wherever you look, there is the manifestation of Allah'.

XVII

Those ulema, those dervishes, and those treading the path of enlightenment, who are not absorbed and have not been benefited by the company of some spiritual guide, they are devoid of the absorption of the secret of Allah. Though they may be dressed in the robe, turban, and dress worn by the Sufis, inwardly they are steeped in greed, lust and carnal desires. Their object, by this dress is not the worship of Allah, but they are through and through seekers of prestige, power and wealth. What is the value of their testimony of faith, their fast and their prayer?

❦ XVIII ❧

If you would like to enter the circle of the enlightened persons, then you must renounce your existence and your self: if you don't denounce and renounce your own self, though you may be dressed as a Sufi, you cannot reach the destination or enter gnosis.

❦ XIX ❧

Those treading the path of enlightenment who are not absorbed cannot attain the gnosis of Allah without the company of the perfect spiritual guide. Neither can they have access to the world of *jabarut* without first replenishing their own self. They remain wandering in the world of *nasut* and *malakut*. They are pleasure seekers and they want name and fame.

❦ XX ❧

A spiritual disciple should not, under any circumstance, hesitate in carrying out the commands of his spiritual guide; whatever he may suggest, any prayer or routine, the disciple should pay his fullest attention to it and should undoubtedly practice it.

The spiritual disciple should, by earnestly following and obeying the spiritual guide, try to reach the place where the spiritual guide himself becomes the comb of his disciple. It should be taken to heart that whatever the spiritual guide persuades his disciple to do and to practice is for the benefit of the spiritual disciple himself. It is imperative upon the spiritual disciple that whatever he may hear from his spiritual teacher and guide he should be attentive to it. Whatever prayers and routine the guide may prescribe for him, he should perform them to the utmost.

❦ XXII ❧

If you sit on the praying carpet after the morning prayers and offer the prayers just after sunrise you will be admitted to heaven. If there are seventy people with you they will all find the gates of heaven open to them.

❦ XXIII ❧

Those in search of Allah have to pass through four stages. The first is that of *shariat*. The next is that of *tariqat*. The third stage is that of *ma'rifat*. When you have proved yourself deserving and acquitted yourself well, and when you have been constant and firm, then alone you will reach the fourth stage, namely that of *haqiqat*. Once you have reached this stage you will get what you ask for.

❦ XXIV ❧

If, after reading the name of Allah and reading the Qur'an your heart is not softened and your faith is not strengthened, but instead you continue to indulge in merry-making, there is no doubt then that it is one of the major sins. If you rise up to it, then you are a believer, and if you fall from the standard, then you are a traitor.

❦ XXV ❧

To see the following six things is a prayer for the mystics:

Firstly, to see your own parents in the morning and to make a salaam to them respectfully.

Secondly, to see your own children with love, blessings and affection is a good type of prayer.

Thirdly, to see the holy Qur'an is itself a prayer. Every possible respect should be shown to the Qur'an.

Fourthly, it is also a prayer to see the face of the learned men with respect. If you have in your heart the love of and regard for the learned ones, then Allah, the Almighty, will confer upon you the rank of a learned one.

Fifthly, it is good to see the gate of Ka'aba. To see the Ka'aba is itself a sort of prayer.

Sixthly, to see towards the face of your own spiritual guide and to be devoted to his service is known as *ma'rifat-al-mureedeen* (gnosis of the spiritual disciples).

❈ XXVI ❈

You should be with your spiritual guide and serve him devotedly and faithfully. If you are not able to do so continuously, then you should do so at least to your utmost capacity and to the best of your means and circumstances.

❈ XXVII ❈

The best type of prayer is:

- To hear the complaints of the aggrieved and to assist them.

- To help the needy and oppressed.
- To feed the hungry.
- To release the captives.

❈ XXVIII ❈

Some people hold the view that there are one hundred stations of *saluk* (the path of spiritual evolution). After covering sixty-nine stations comes the station of supernatural powers. The wayfarer in this particular path should not exhibit his supernatural powers unless and until he has crossed the seventy stations. But it is better that they should be exhibited only after covering the hundred stations.

Some people belonging to the Chishti order have fixed fifteen stations of spiritual evolution and out of these fifteen there are five stations pertaining to supernatural powers. The Chishti Khawajas hold that the one who treads the path should not stop after only these five stations, but he should with courage and determination cross all the fifteen stations. Afterwards he is allowed to exhibit his supernatural powers, so that he may be counted as perfect among the perfect ones.

❈ XXIX ❈

A saintly man explained the meaning of 'non-existence' and 'to be everlasting' thus: 'When I took the world to be my enemy and severed my relations with the people of the world, I paid the fullest uninterrupted attention to the Creator, then the love of Allah so overwhelmed me that I took even myself as an enemy. I found death to be removed from in-between. Then I derived the pleasure of everlasting life. The love of Allah then became manifest to me.'

❧ XXX ☙

On the Day of Judgement the lovers will receive the command of Allah to enter paradise. Paradise should be given to those who have prayed and remembered Him for the sake of paradise and its comforts. Their only object is nothing but the Friend.

❧ XXXI ☙

You should, if possible, try to know the secret of everlasting life. If not it is better for you to be devoted to piety. Many found themselves helpless in that path and many a helpless one was made to traverse this path by none other than the saints.

❧ XXXII ☙

Allah has made his lovers content and happy by His friendship and love. Due to this they are silent and devoted to Allah alone. They have nothing to do with the desires and pleasures of life. They are not aware of the things of the world. They are people of lofty ideals.

❧ XXXIII ☙

The one whose heart is absorbed in the love of Allah does not feel restless. So it is incumbent upon the lover of Allah that he should be indifferent to both the worlds; if he acts otherwise then he is not a true lover.

❦ XXXIV ❧

When Allah brought Adam into existence He said to him: 'Pray! In other words, remember me in thy heart. Know me to be present in thy body. Give place to My love in the head I have created thee for this purpose, that thou may'st know Me, glorify Me, and love Me.'

❦ XXXV ❧

The trust reposed by the God-illumined men in Allah should be such that they need not seek help from anyone, nor should they look towards anyone, nor should they pay any attention to anyone, except to Allah, the Supreme, Who is omnipotent and omnipresent.

❦ XXXVI ❧

When Adam incurred the displeasure of Allah then his stick and everything else besides, wept - except for silver and gold. Allah asked them why they did not weep. Thereupon silver and gold asked: 'Why should we weep for the one who has incurred Thy displeasure?' Then Allah said: 'I swear by my Glory and Might that I shall make manifest your utility, grandeur and power to the children of Adam. I shall make them your slaves.'

❦ XXXVII ❧

On the Day of Judgement, if, when the true lovers are called, one amongst them were to react, establishing his claim to be a lover of Allah, he would undoubtedly forfeit his claim of being sincere and constant in his love. He would feel ashamed. He would have to hide his face from the true lovers. A voice would come out to the effect: 'Those claimants of love are not real lovers. Remove them from amongst Our lovers'.

❈ XXXVIII ❈

Repentance is of three kinds so far as the mystics are concerned. Firstly to eat less in order to fulfill the obligations of the fast; secondly, to sleep less in order to worship; thirdly to speak less in order to pray. First comes fear, next comes hope, and last comes love. Under the heading of fear comes the avoidance of sin, so that the hell-fire may be avoided. Under hope comes the necessity of prayers, in order to get paradise and the desire to reach the destination in order to achieve immortal life. Under love comes contemplation in order to get the divine pleasure.

❈ XXXIX ❈

It is of utmost importance in the spiritual domain that you should repose implicit confidence and faith in your spiritual guide and teacher.

❈ XL ❈

There are three things that go to make an enlightened person - namely fear, respect, and shyness.

Fear to him means that he is ever and anon ashamed of his shortcomings. Respect to him means that he devotes himself exclusively to prayers. Shyness to him means that he does not cast his looks on anyone else except Allah, the All-pervading.

❈ XLI ❈

A spiritual disciple should follow his spiritual teacher faithfully and devotedly. He should carry out the behest of his spiritual teacher so that he may attain perfection.

❈ XLII ❈

If you want to be free from the hell-fire and the fear of the Day of Resurrection, you should obey Allah. You should obey Him in those details that are superior to any prayer, namely to do justice to the aggrieved, to help the helpless, and to feed the hungry.

❈ XLIII ❈

The repentance of the lovers is of three kinds. Firstly shame, secondly avoidance of sins, thirdly to purify themselves by purging cruelty and enmity from within themselves.

❈ XLIV ❈

The things necessary for a dervish are: search for God; search for the spiritual guide and teacher; respect; surrender, love; piety; constancy; perseverance, to eat less ; to sleep less; seclusion; prayer and fast.

❈ XLV ❈

For a mystic the necessary things are:

- to be perfect in divine knowledge
- to be neither sorry nor sad himself, nor to make others sorry or sad and not to think evil of anybody;

- to point the way to Allah and to lead and guide the people towards the ultimate good;
- to be hospitable;
- to prefer seclusion;
- to pay respect and regard to everyone and to count himself as the humblest and the lowest;
- to surrender his will to the Will of Allah, the Almighty;
- to be patient and persevering in every sorrow, grief and woe;
- to be humble and meek;
- to be contented and to repose trust in Allah

❈ XLVI ❈

Among the people of the world they are indeed the wisest who have taken to mysticism and renunciation, because here the object is to have no object and to lose the object is to gain the object. Contrary to this those in ignorance have taken happiness as trouble and have treated trouble as happiness.

❈ XLVII ❈

He indeed is the wisest who upon the mere thought of some worldly object renounces it then and there and accepts faqr (poverty) and renunciation as his ultimate goal. Thus renouncing and foregoing all his desires he finds himself in accord with renunciation.

❈ XLVIII ❈

Prayer forms the chief ascension. Once a man knowing it proceeds with sincerity he becomes so thirsty it is as if he has taken several cups of fire. The more cups he takes the more thirsty he becomes because the glory of the Unlimited knows no limits. At that time his harmony becomes disharmony and his comfort becomes discomfort, unless he feels honoured and blessed by the glorious vision of Allah.

❈ XLIX ❈

If you want to understand and appreciate the secrets and implications of mysticism you should close the door of comfort upon yourself and then sit cross legged, being enamoured of love. If you have done this you will become a mystic indeed.

*The Meditations
of
Khawaja Muinuddin Hasan Chishti*

Part Three

Manifestations

Manifestations

The path of love is such that if you tread on it you will lose your name and identity.

Whosoever gained anything gained it by service.

Prayer is of great necessity for the development of the soul.

Prayer is a secret and a mystery which man confides to Allah.

Except in prayer there is no other opportunity available to express one's own secret (to Allah).

Prayer for the people is a trust of Allah. Men then should try to acquit themselves well.

Those believers are really to be pitied who do not offer prayers at the right time and woe to them who do not follow the worship of Allah.

If you wish to protect yourself from hellfire then you should try to discharge your duties of worship and prayer to Allah.

There is no better thing before Allah than prayer.

The perfect and the sincere seekers don't enter into arguments. Instead they are silent and respectful.

The nearness of Allah cannot be obtained without being in the company of the perfect spiritual guide and teacher.

The heart of a *mumin* (believer) has at all times within it the silent remembrance of Allah. Hence he gets everlasting life.

The heart of a common Muslim is unmindful of the remembrance of Allah. Hence he is dead.

The prophets and saints are ever engaged in the silent remembrance of Allah.

The secret remembrance and the real prayer constitute the renunciation of the self.

It is through love that *fana* (annihilation of the self) is achieved. the one who has become the lover of Allah is absorbed in Allah and lost in Allah. The one who is so united with Allah becomes a mirror of Allah.

Allah says: 'O, ye people! I am within you. Why do you not see Me?' Since Allah lives in the heart, the heart is the throne and the abode of Allah.

In the phantom of the dust He it is Who speaks, Who hears, and Who sees. He is the one Who guides and leads.

The gift of the divine secret is not given to the undeserving masses.

The one who feeds the hungry is freed from the horrors of hell. Allah fulfils his thousand wants.

To make a false oath is to ruin your own house. The house is deprived of benevolence and blessings.

It is a sin in the fourth station of *saluk* (spiritual travel) if when you hear the name of Allah or the holy Qur'an your heart be not softened and your faith be not strengthened due to the majesty of Allah.

Allah controls everything. You should not hesitate in carrying out His commands.

Obedience to the command of Allah will secure for you whatever you command.

The worship of the enlightened one is *commemoratio cordis* remembrance of heart.

When Allah, the Almighty, created Adam He said to him 'Pray!' When Adam prostrated his heart was engaged in love, his soul attained nearness, and his head got union.

When the enlightened one casts his look upon the world of unity and upon the majesty of the divine glory, then he becomes blind, so that he may not look towards others.

It is the motto of the enlightened ones that belief is a light, by which a person is illumined.

Without the angel of death the world is not worth a handful of barley. As to why, in the traditions it is given that, 'Death is a bridge and passing across it the friend is united with the Friend'.

He is the weakest person indeed who does not stick to his word.

The world is mortal and its engagements are of no use.

A dervish is one who does not need anything and does not hanker after anything except His everlasting beauty, for all the creation is a mirror and a manifestation of His everlasting beauty. Hence he sees his object in all things.

A seeker should ever and anon pursue faithfully and diligently his object. You should know what is the object. Let it be known that the object is the same pain and anguish whether it be *haqiqi* (real) or *majazi* (non-real). Here, by the 'non-real anguish', is meant the beginning of the commands of the *shariat*.

The enlightened person in fact becomes a sovereign. Neither does he expect anything from anyone nor is he afraid of anyone. Allah says of such people: 'The saints have no fear and no grief'.

Prayer is the medium through which the service of Allah is acquired.

The enlightened person is one who renounces both the worlds and thus frees himself.

If you feed the hungry, you earn blessings for yourself. Your act of charity in feeding the hungry creates seven curtains between yourself and hell.

If you swear falsely, you will bring evil and disgrace not only upon yourself but also on the other inmates of your household. The house is then deprived of the blessings of Allah.

Loud laughter is one of the sins itself.

You should not laugh at all in a graveyard.

A graveyard is a place where you can learn a lesson. It is not a place for merry-making. O my dear! The more you are engrossed in worldly affairs the more remote you are from Allah. If you are as much busy in your appointed task, namely the remembrance of Allah, as you are in worldly affairs, then so much the better for you.

The closer you come to the people of the world, the more detached you are from Allah.

We have to go on the great journey. We should all try to equip ourselves properly for the same.

There is perhaps no greater sin than causing injury to the believers without reason. To do so is surely to displease the holy Prophet Muhammad.

The lover and the Beloved are indeed one and the same. All this is the glory of the One. In other words the One saw the One.

No sin is greater and more harmful than inflicting an injury, giving harm to and putting in disgrace your own brother Muslim.

The religious dignitaries, having vast knowledge to their credit, will have no knowledge, learning or piety with them on their entering paradise. But the godly men and the saints will carry with them, even in heaven, their characteristic mark of love!

The society of the good is better than doing good work, whereas the society of the bad is worse than doing bad work.

The God-illuminated man disdains the world for there is nothing in the world except enmity and jealousy. Consequently the one devoted to the world is far from Allah.

In the path of spiritual illumination one can see everything. When a man reaches close to Allah and he derives the pleasure of union, then of course he stops weeping (the weeping due to separation).

Blessed are those dervishes of this time, who sit together and show to each other mutual love and sincerity, for thus they acquire inner purity.

Bad indeed are those dervishes who do not meet each other and keep themselves aloof. This is a bad thing.

The Day of Judgement is a certainty.

The lover's heart is a fireplace of love. Whatever comes into it is burnt and becomes annihilated.

The noise of the lover is before he sees his Beloved. Once he sees His Beloved he becomes calm and quiet, just as the rivers are boisterous before they join the ocean, but when they have joined the ocean, they are becalmed forever.

Those indeed are lovers of Allah who, if they offer the morning prayer are continuously in the thought of the Friend, till the next morning prayer.

There are such lovers of Allah, whom the love of Allah has made quiet to such an extent that they do not know whether there is anything else existing in the world.

You are indeed a true lover of Allah, when you renounce from your heart the idea of both the worlds.

You are a true lover of Allah when you welcome with delight the sorrows and pain received from the Friend.

You are only a true lover of Allah when you sever your bonds of love from your parents, brothers, and sons and devote yourself exclusively to Allah and His Prophet.

The lovers of Allah hear the talk of the Friend directly.

There is no fire greater in its intensity than the fire of love.

To be obedient and to be afraid of the Friend is the sign of love indeed.

When you enter on the path of love of the Friend you become non-existent.

When you have love in your heart you don't feel the least troubled by poverty, hunger, or asceticism.

He is in a prison house indeed who claims to be pious.

Be ever prepared for death.

The enlightened person is one whose heart is a stranger to all save Allah.

The enlightened person is one who is indifferent to both the worlds, this world and the world hereafter.

The heart of the enlightened person should be such that he may efface everything and may be exclusively devoted to the glorious vision of the Friend.

The enlightened person is one who does not keep anything dear to his heart, except the remembrance of Allah.

The enlightened person is an enemy of the world and a friend of Allah. That is why he renounces the world and is above the trifles of life.

The enlightened person is one who does not implore help from anyone except Allah.

The enlightened person becomes perfect only when all else is removed from between him and the Friend. Either he remains or the Friend.

The pinnacle of the enlightened person is that he may ever feel restless in the love of the Friend.

The enlightened person is one who removes from his heart all else so that he may become one, particularly single, like his Friend.

The enlightened person is one whose morning is unacquainted with his nightly works and deeds.

The meditation of the enlightened person must be so deep as to dispel every memory of the past.

An enlightened person is one who receives every day, from the All-high, a hundred thousand visions and in every minute a few thousand. He thus receives spiritual ecstasy every moment.

The enlightened person is one who, if he receives a hundred visions, may not disclose them all.

To produce in someone the attributes of Allah is indeed humblest thing that the enlightened person can do. The greatest thing that the enlightened person can do is to make the one who comes before him with a claim feel guilty by his own spiritual powers. [*In other words he makes the one coming before him feel guilty because he realises that he was in fact not trying to acquire the attributes of Allah.*]The trust reposed by the enlightened person in Allah is such that it is as if he is bewildered.

The enlightened person is one who acquires all knowledge, gives a myriad of meanings and every time dips deep into the ocean of meanings, so that he may take out from it the jewel of the divine light. He may show such a jewel to the expert jewellers so that they may like him and come to know him as one amongst the enlightened ones.

The enlightened person does not repose his trust in anybody except Allah. Accordingly he does not pay attention to anyone beside Allah.

It is characteristic of the enlightened person that he is ever smiling. When he smiles the angels come before him, and seeing the angels he continues smiling.

The enlightened person, like the sun, showers his rays of light on all the world. the whole world is lit bright by his light.

The eyes of the perfect enlightened one sees all that is in your fate.

The hallmark of the enlightened person is this, that he keeps his death dear to his heart, renounces the pleasures of life and derives comfort and solace by the remembrance of Allah alone.

The least thing that the enlightened person does is that he disdains wealth and splendour.

The contented person indeed is the one who does not complain to anybody of any grievous wrong, pain, or sorrow caused by the people.

A dervish should be so close to Allah that He may give him whatever he may want. If not, then he is not entitled to be called a dervish.

Whoever got any blessings got them by generosity alone.

There is a time in the life of the contented when they are enamoured of love alone. If then they are torn asunder they are quite unaware of it.

The spiritual disciple deserves to be called a dervish only when he lives in the world of non-existence.

In the world there is nothing better than the company of the mystics and the respect shown to the saints.

If the people of the world come to know even a little of those sleeping under the ground, they will undoubtedly become motionless and would dissolve like salt in water.

It is incumbent upon an individual to be devoted to Allah alone, who is everlasting and eternal.

If Allah, the Almighty, be pleased to give eyes to one then one should be content to see nothing except Him, the All-pervading.

You may find the great reality hidden in whatsoever you see in both the worlds.

Every particle of dust is a cup wherein the entire world can be seen.

The one who has come to realise Allah does not ask anything and renounces all his desires and wishes.

If you have not realized Allah you cannot understand such people.

It is necessary to renounce greed and avarice. If you have done so you will attain the object.

The heart which Allah has switched off from Himself should be wrapped up in a coffin of passions and be buried deep beneath the ground of shame.

The enlightened person on attaining the stage of perfection performs a difficult task of the highest order at that time. That is prayer with utmost sincerity. Thus, through this, he attains nearness and vision.

When all things other than Allah are effaced and removed from the heart, then alone is the object achieved.

Mysticism is a name and not a custom.

The Sufis breathe nothing but love.

Chronology of Khawaja Muinuddin Hasan Chishti

530AH/1135AD   Born in Isfahan, brought up in Sanjar. Son of Khawaja Ghiyasuddin Hasan and Bibi Mah Nur. He had two brothers.

544AH/1150AD   The death of his father. A grinding stone and a garden formed part of his inheritance. Meets a mystic named Ibrahim Qandoozi, who offers him a piece of oil cake that brought about a noticeable change in his condition. Sold his grinding stone and the garden. Left in search of truth. Reaches Khorasan. Stays in Samarqand and Bukhara for five years receiving education.

550AH/1156AD   Leaves Samarqand and Bukhara.

551AH/1156AD   Meets Hazrat Mohiuddin Abdul Qadir of Jilan (better known as Ghous-ul-Azam). Leaves Iraq for Arabia. Returns from Arabia and undertakes a journey to Harun (Haroon). Passes two and a half years in the company of Khawaja Uthman of Harun.

555AH/1160AD. Visits Baghdad where he meets Shaykh Abu Najeeb Suhrawardy. Leaves Baghdad for Syria.

556AH/1161AD. Kirman visited.

557AH/1162AD   Visits Hamdan, Tabriz, Bukhara, Kharqan, and Samarqand.

558AH/1163AD   Visits Memna.

560AH/1165AD   Visits Herat.

561AH/1165AD   Arrives in India for the first time. Visits Multan. Proceeds to Lahore where he spent two weeks at the tomb of Sheikh Ali Hujwiri, better known as Data Ganj Baksh.

Proceeds to Ghazni, Balkh, Astrabad and Merv. Returns to Baghdad and accompanies Khawaja Uthman Haruni on his travels.

562AH/1166AD   Meets Sheikh Shahabuddin Suhrawardy in Baghdad. Leaves Baghdad for Mecca with his spiritual guide Khawaja Uthman Haruni. Reaches Falooja and Mecca.

Honoured by the visit to the Kaaba. Reached Medina where he offered himself at the court of the holy Prophet Muhammad. Reaches Oosh where he meets Sheikh Bahauddin.

Goes to Badakshan and Bukhara.

573AH/1177AD   Qutubuddin Bakhtiyar Kaka sent by his mother to Khawaja Muinuddin Hasan Chishti for the former's 'Bismillah' ceremony (though it was actually performed by Qazi Hamiduddin Nagore). Sewistan visited where he meets Sadiuddin Muhammad Ahmed.

581AH/1185AD   Meets Sheikh Najrauddin Kubra in Sanjar. Meets Sheikh Abdul Qadir al-Jillani for a second time.

582AH/1186AD   Receives the holy relics and is appointed spiritual successor by his spiritual guide.

583AH/1187AD   Reaches Oosh and moves on to Isfahan. Accepts Khawaja Qutubuddin Bakhtiyar Kaki as his disciple. Leaves Isfahan for Mecca to perform the pilgrimage.

After performing the pilgrimage proceeds to Medina. Receives a mandate from the holy Prophet to proceed to Ajmer.

586AH/1190AD   Reaching Baghdad from Medina, appoints Khawaja Qutubuddin Kaki as his Caliph and Sajjadanashin. Reaches Chisht, and proceeds to Subzawar. Yadgar Muhammad becomes a disciple.

587AH/1191AD   Reaches Lahore via Multan.Proceeds to Delhi. Stays in Samana from where he proceeds to Ajmer. Reaches Ajmer for the first time. Sadhu Ram and Ajai Pal enter his fold. Muhammad Yadgar sent to select a place for residence. Leaves Ajmer.

588AH/1191AD. Ajmer revisited - coming from Ghazni via Lahore and Delhi.

590AH/1194AD   His first marriage with Bibi Ummat Ullah.Two sons born out of this union, namely Khawaja Fakhruddin A'bul Khair and Khawaja Hissamuddin. Also a daughter named Bibi Hafiz Jamal.

598AH/1200AD   Leaves Ajmer for Baghdad. Visits Balkh. Maulana Ziauddin becomes his follower.

602AH/1206AD   Visits Ajmer a third time, reaching from Balkh via Ghazni, Lahore and Delhi.

610AH/1213AD   Arrives in India for the fifth time and in Ajmer for the fourth time.

611AH/1214AD   Arrives in Delhi, during the reign of Sultan Iltutmish, for the first time.

611AH/1215AD   Confers a robe on Baba Fariduddin Ganj-i-Shakar. Khawaja Uthman Haruni arrives in Delhi. Writes a book entitled 'Kanjul Israr' at the behest of his spiritual guide.

615AH/1219AD   Returns from Delhi to Ajmer

.620AH/1223AD Marries a second time to Bibi Asmat Ullah. Out of this union, Khawaja Ziauddin Abu Said born.

621AH/1224AD   Visits Delhi a second time during the reign of Sultan Iltutmish, to plead on behalf of a farmer. Returns to Ajmer.

627AH/1229AD   Bids Khawaja Qutubuddin Bakhtiyar Kaki, who is with him in Ajmer, farewell

Breathes his last. Tomb in Ajmer.

The Message of Khawaja Uthman Harooni -
The Spiritual Guide of Khawaja Muinuddin Hasan Chishti

Preface

Just imagine that you are sitting at the feet of a Sufi Shaykh. You may ask him about Sufism – the mystical path of Islam – and perhaps you want to know what a Sufi is. He will answer that Sufism is the spiritual path towards God. A Sufi is the one who travels on this path. A Sufi is a lover of God who, by means of love and devotion moves towards his Beloved

Perhaps the Sufi Sheikh will use the example of the rose. As you know the rose is the symbol of love and Sufism can be explained through the allegory of a rose. The thorn of the rose is the symbol of the outward or religious knowledge (Shariat). Its stem stands for the mystical path of inner knowledge (Tariqat). The flower may be compared with supernatural knowledge (Marifat) and the scent of the rose with knowledge of the Truth (Haqiqat). The thorn refers to the difficulties on the spiritual path. All Sufis will tell you that it is very important to be guided by an experienced Murshid (spiritual teacher). Khawaja Hafiz Shirazi clearly says:

In love's domain,
Do not take one step without a guide,
For on this road,
He who has no guide loses his way.

That is why the first step in Sufism is the initiation in one of the Sufi Orders. The Sufi Sheikhs train their murids (disciples) in a way that is consistent with their capacities. One person has to fast, the next gets instructions in regard to meditation and a third has to perform a certain Dhikr (invocation or remembrance of God). One murid (disciple) may be advised to keep aloof from the world, another may receive the injunction to succeed in the world. There are several Sufi orders in existence, like e.g. the Chishti order, the Qadiri and the Naqshbandi brotherhoods. The Chishti Order was founded by Hazrat Abu Ishaq Shami Chishti (d. 965 A.D.) The Sufis of this order emphasise the importance of the love of God. By means of love the limitations of the ego are removed and direct observation of The Reality is made possible. It has been said:

For those who love Him,
He alone is their joy and sorrow,
He alone is their recompense and reward.
If anyone other than the Beloved is seen,
Then that is not love, it is mere passion.
Love is that flame which, when it blazes up,
Consumes all but the Beloved Himself.

The Qadiri Order, founded by Sheikh Abdul Qadir al-Jilani (1098-1187) lays stress on the emptying the inward faculties from all thoughts other than God. Spiritual practices such as Dhikr (remembrance of God) are the means to achieve the necessary purification.

Sufism cannot be learnt from books. One has to follow the training of a spiritual guide. This book is an experiment as it is a word by word recoding of a teaching session. Some time ago Hazrat Zahur ul Hassan Sharib, the present Sheikh of the Gudri Shah Order of the Sufis gave a speech on All India

Radio which is here made available for non-Urdu speaking murids (disciples) and others interested.

The way of teaching of the Sufis is very often an indirect one. They may refer to the life and teachings of some great Sufi master of the past. The one listening to these teaching stories may get out of it what is in it for him or her. That is why Hazrat Zahur ul Hassan Sharib (1914-1996) spoke about Khawaja Uthman Harooni, one of the prominent saints of the Chishti Order.

In reading this book it is important to keep in mind that it is the presentation of a talk of a Sufi Sheikh. It is one thing to hear about a rose but it is better to see the rose and best to smell the rose. So remember this; you are listening to a Sufi Sheikh who is speaking about a rose.....

From the original preface by Mohammed Siraj

His Life

Many search but few find happiness and peace of mind. How many people can claim to be leading a better life? I think very few people can claim that they are leading a better life. What is a 'better life' after all? A better life implies the spirit of help, mutual help, understanding, mutual understanding, regard and mutual regard. If these qualities are cultivated I think there will be peace in the world and peace in the country. All those invidious distinctions of caste, communalism, religion, and region will be automatically removed and our world will become a better place to live in.

To make the world a better place to live in was the one concern of Hazrat Khawaja Uthman Harooni.

The day I spoke on All-India Radio from the Jaipur station it was about Khawaja Uthman Harooni, and perhaps you know that he is the spiritual guide and teacher of the great saint Khawaja Moinuddin Hasan Chishti. As a matter fact Khawaja Uthman Harooni doesn't require any tribute praise or introduction. For his greatness and eminence it is enough that he is the spiritual guide o the towering saint Khawaja Moinuddin Hasan Chishti.

He trained him in such a fashion and in such a way that he was enabled to found a spiritual kingdom which is still existing, living and growing. It is such a spiritual kingdom on which the sun does not set.

Hazrat Khawaja Uthman Harooni was the spiritual disciple of Hazrat Khawaja Haji Sharif Zindani who was a very eminent saint belonging to the Chishti Order. Like his spiritual ancestors Khawaja Uthman Harooni also began to be called Chishti. He was born in Haroon (Iran). Since he was born there he became known as Harooni (of Haroon).

As is the custom amongst Muslims when he attained the age of four years, four months, and four days his Bismillah was performed. Bismillah means a function celebrating the occasion of a child commencing school for the first time. He was sent to a Maktab a school where, shortly, he acquired knowledge and learning and also committed the Holy Qur'an to memory. The one who commits the Holy Qur'an to memory is known as Hafiz.

His meeting with an absorbed person, I mean a *Majzub*, was a turning point in his life. The name of that absorbed person was Chirk. He was a very, very absorbed person always lost in himself. The close association of Khawaja Uthman Harooni with that *Majzub* brought about a change and a transformation in his life. Khawaja Uthman Harooni felt disgusted with mundane affairs. He took the world to be a child's game in which children play and then retire. For him life lost its charm. He wanted to embrace a different type of life; one that could confer upon him higher moral and spiritual values. In this search he greatly succeeded.

He had heard of the name Hazrat Hajji Sharif Zindani. He went to him and entreated him to enrol him as a disciple. Khawaja Hajji Sharif Zindani finding him a fit and proper person accepted him and with his own hand placed upon his head the four-edged cap. Placing the cap on his head he explained its implications. He told him that the four-edged cap implied the following four things:

First is the renunciation of the world:

Second is the renunciation of the world hereafter:

Third is the renunciation of the desires of the self:

Fourth is renunciation of everything other than God.

Khawaja Uthman Harooni lived in his company for over thirty years. During this time he was engaged in ascetic practices and in prayers. Time rolled on and he acquired great spiritual accomplishments. After that his spiritual guide allowed him to go and preach the gospel of truth. He undertook tours and travels and visited many countries and cities. Among them may be mentioned Bukhara, Baghdad, Falooja, Damascus, Mecca and Medina. He also performed Hajj – the annual pilgrimage enjoined by Islam. On the way to Mecca he reached a city where he saw a group of Dervishes absorbed in and intoxicated with the love of God. He stayed there for sometime but those Dervishes did not regain consciousness. On reaching Falooja he stayed in a secluded place in a Mosque and he offered his respects at the shrine of the holy Prophet Mohammed. He travelled to Bukhara where he met the outstanding Sufi saints there. On the way to Oosh he met Sheikh Bahauddin of Oosh.

Subsequently He arrived at Badakshan. There he met a saintly man who was one of the attendants of Hazrat Junayd of Baghdad. He was about a hundred years old and one of his feet had been amputated. Upon being questioned about this he said that it had so happened that one day, in order to give some relief to himself, he took his foot out of the secluded place he had chosen for himself. As soon as he took his foot out he heard a voice admonishing him and asking if this was the promise he had forgot so soon. When he heard the voice he felt ashamed and guilty. His feelings of shame and guilt prompted him to cut off his foot which he did. This had happened forty years ago and since then he had been wondering how he would show his face to the dervishes on the Day of Judgement.

Returning to Baghdad he stayed there for some time. During all this time his very close and dear spiritual disciple Khawaja Muinuddin Hasan Chishti was always with him. He was with him for long over twenty-two years, carrying his tiffin basket for him.

After some time he thought of visiting India and did so during the reign of Emperor Shamsuddin Altamish, who is generally called Il Tut Mish. He was a god-fearing king and he was very fond of the company of dervishes. The impact of his previous life in Baghdad was prominently displayed in his character.

Baghdad in those days was the seat not only of knowledge and learning and erudition but it was also the seat of Sufism. The saints belonging to the Chishti and Qadiri orders lived, preached and exhorted the people to embrace a nobler and better type of life. There were many mosques, very many good mosques. Among them the mosque of Abul Lais Samarqandi and the mosque of Junayd of Baghdad were the outstanding reminders of that piety and holiness that had contributed to a better style of life.

There was also a turning point for Il Tut Mish. Perhaps you may know that he was a slave. In Baghdad he was serving his own master. One day his master sent him to fetch some grapes. He lost the money and was standing on the roadside weeping. In the meanwhile a dervish passed that way and asked him the reason for his weeping. He explained his master had given him money and he had lost it. He feared when he returned he would be punished. The dervish consoled him and gave him money with which to purchase grapes and he returned home happily. But before he could leave the dervish the dervish asked that, should he ever attain eminence and assumed the reins sovereignty he should not forget dervishes and should ever take it as his humble and pleasant duty to serve them. This Il Tut Mish sincerely followed.

When Hazrat Khawaja Uthman reached Delhi Il Tut Mish immediately went and offered his respects and regards and sat before him with folded hands to express his regard and respect for the great saint. He entreated him to accept him as one of his disciples. Hazrat Khawaja Uthman Harooni was pleased with his pleasant manners. He accepted him as one of his disciples and for his guidance and his study he asked Khawaja Muinuddin Hasan Chishti to write a book based on Qur'anic verses and on Hadith and the teachings of the saints, which was to serve as a guide book for Sultan Il Tut Mish so that he may not be lost in the labyrinth of carnal desires.

After staying for a long while in Delhi, and after conferring his multifarious and many blessings on the king and the high and low he left Delhi. After leaving Delhi he led a retired life and ultimately it so happened that the desire of a friend to meet his Friend overtook him.

He died on the 5th Shawwal in the year 617 A.H. (1220 A.D.) His tomb in Mecca is an object of adoration and dedication to thousands of people belonging to every strata of society and to every school of thought.

As regards the place of Hazrat Khawaja Uthman Harooni in the galaxy of saints, I will say without fear of contradiction that he stands as an eminent and shining star. His greatness lies in that he lived as a saint, worked as a saint, and died as a saint. There was no contradiction in his life. He was a man of simple living and high thinking. His wants were few and his desires were few. He just lived as a man of mission would live. For seventy long years he did not eat to his heart's content and he did not sleep for the whole night.

He was always a pillar of strength and a source of inspiration to the needy, the handicapped and to those in trouble. People would come to him and when they were in distress or when they were faced by some trial or tribulation they automatically looked towards him and took him as their friend and as their philosopher.

His Message

As I have just indicated Hazrat Khawaja Uthman Harooni was a man with a mission. It was in pursuance of this mission that he took great pains; pains for the betterment of humanity at large. He envisaged a society in which there was no exploitation, but exploitation was replaced by cooperation. He believed, and firmly believed, that a man should live and let others live. He did not want that those enemies that are besieging an individual should ever be with him. He exhorted the people that they should get rid of greed, lust for power, lust for fame, lust for money, or lust for wealth. On the contrary their desires should be to obtain piety, more piety, and nothing but piety.

To him a great man was one who was endowed with a higher quality of inner virtues – virtues like contentment, virtues like sincerity, virtues like self-abnegation, self sacrifice, and above all the spirit of renunciation. The ego in man according to him was itself an enemy that did not allow man to think rationally, act wisely and to live happily. He also exhorted the people that Love should be placed in a beautiful case – rather a beautiful frame, as it was a beautiful gift given by God. He also emphasised that unless a man loves human beings it is impossible for that person to love God.

He asked the people in their own way to remember God. The world is in fact nothing but the forgetfulness of God. A man may live in the world, follow his vocation or profession or his daily duty; he may be leading a family life, he may have a wife, he may have children, he may have a business, he may have a profession, he may have a vocation, but if he is not unmindful of God he cannot be said to be a man of the world. As soon as he forgets God he becomes a creature, a slave of the world. So the world means a man once he forgets God – that is world.

That is his contribution and that is his unique thought that changed, moulded and shaped the lives of so many people who had heard his message or had had the occasion to read teachings, precepts and sayings or his aphorisms and advice.

His advice was one word and that was:- 'Live'. This means that to live is one thing and to exist is another thing. There are so many people, rather unfortunate people, who do not live but who merely exist. To exist means a man is breathing but to live is different. He exhorted the people saying that living required that the man should be a type of man that has not his own personal interests in view but is interested in others. A self-centred man cannot be said to be living a good life. He emphasised that to earn a good life requires one's own efforts. No exterior agency, no legislation, no act (of government) can make a man moral. It is by one's own serious efforts that he comes to live. The one who has learned to live has discovered his own (higher) Self.

Inner discovery is a very important thing in Sufism. So many people have been thinking they are living but they have not shown signs of organism and growth, which means they have not been helpful to others. They have not shared the burden of others and they have not been helping themselves. A sick man cannot attend another man. They were like sick men and they were living in the hospital called world.

Khawaja Uthman Harooni was, in fact, a vision to the people. It has been said, I think I read somewhere, that where there is no vision the people perish [*Proverbs 29.18*]. In fact he was a vision but at the same time he was not a visionary. It is true he had the idealism of a saint. This idealism prompted him to undertake the gigantic task of the reconstruction of humanity. He himself by precept and practice showed the way of enlightenment. He showed the path where a person can seek his own salvation by his own unaided efforts.

Khawaja Uthman Harooni was an emblem and an epitaph of a life nobly lived. He showed the marvellous traits of contentment, hope, belief and faith. To him faith was a pillar of strength. A man of faith was a man who had a strong backing behind him. In times of difficulty, in times of stress, in times of anxiety or in times strain and stress, when a man loses his mental equilibrium or mental balance, it is faith in him that gives him energy, vitality and force; and keeps him in a good state. Faith is a very good guide, a very good friend and a very good helper.

Khawaja Uthman Harooni stood for social justice. He wanted that the people should enjoy equal opportunities. It was not the lot of the common man to suffer and neither was it the fortune of the upper or middle class to live in affluence and to deny the same kind of life to their brethren who were in adversity, who were leading a life of of hardship, who were groaning, moaning, weeping and shedding tears.

He advocated and at the same time emphasised that people should come together and not live in isolation, for the simple reason that those in isolation assume superiority complex. Amongst the Sufis it has not been the practice to live in an ivory tower and ignore the realities of the world. They face and they accept every challenge that may come their way. If a man is cowed down by the everyday toils and by the challenge that he receives from different quarters then the man is not only lost to himself but he is lost to the world at large.

Khawaja Uthman Harooni was a humanist, but this humanism was born of a desire to raise the standard of living and to lead the people to the fountain of contentment and happiness, prosperity and bliss. The time in which he lived was a turbulent time. Society was seething with faction and discontent. People felt insecure. They were at variance. There were wars; there were conquests; there was plunder. In such an atmosphere people had neither inner peace nor outer security. The result was that pessimism had seized the people and it was his greatest contribution that he changed the atmosphere of pessimism into one of optimism. A Sufi saint has always an optimistic outlook and he was no exception. He always stood by the masses. He always helped his murids (spiritual disciples) in whatever way he could. He stood by them through thick and thin.

In order to help his murids Khawaja Uthman Harooni gave discourses at times which may guide them.

Once he disclosed the secret that when the Friend becomes your friend then the whole universe in fact becomes yours – but it is necessary that you should be unmindful of everything else; be ever with the Friend and follow Him faithfully and assiduously.

At another time he showed contempt for those mendicants who ate to their hearts content and took themselves to be mendicant and wore the Khirqa – the robe of the dervishes.

Distinguishing between *Shariat* (the revealed law of Islam) and *Tariqat*, the mode of worship of the Sufis, he said that in *shariat* wine is forbidden but in *Tariqat* it is not allowed to drink water to the heart's content, for by doing so one becomes lazy in offering prayers.

According to him a *Momin* (one of the faithful) is one who keeps three things dear to his heart: firstly mendicancy, secondly illness and thirdly death.

To him – he indeed is the spiritual son (murid) who gives a high place to the teachings and precepts of his Murshid (spiritual guide) – and practices them faithfully.

Once he said that Hazrat Ali had disclosed that he heard from the holy Prophet Muhammad that a woman who is obedient to her husband shall enter heaven with Bibi Fatima (the Holy Prophet's daughter).

He deprecated weeping and wailing in times of difficulty. He said that Hazrat Abdullah Ansari had said that the Holy prophet Muhammad laid down that the one who weeps and wails in times of trouble and tribulation invites the curse of God on himself.

He holds that one who feeds the hungry – God fulfils his one thousand wants and frees him from hellfire. For him a house is built in heaven.

According to him he who gives food to a Dervish becomes free from all sins.

Supernatural Events

One day it so happened that one of his spiritual disciples came to Khawaja Uthman. The disciple was very sorry and sad. He was dejected, dismayed and desperate and his condition was evident from his face. As soon as the disciple reached his presence Khawaja Uthman Harooni looked towards him and asked as to what was the reason for his being so engulfed in gloom. The man with tears in his eyes submitted that nothing was hidden from his holiness and that he was in fact in great mental perturbation and distress. He said: 'It has so happened your holiness that my immediate neighbour has built a two-story house. When he goes to the upper storey it becomes difficult for my women folk to come out and sit in the courtyard. I asked him not to do so but he insisted in doing this with the result that if I keep quiet I suffer the agony, if I speak there is a possibility of picking a quarrel with my neighbour.'

Then Khawaja Uthman asked him; 'Tell me does your neighbour know that you are one of my disciples?' Upon this he replied, 'Surely sir, he knows i am your slave and that I have the honour and privilege of kissing your threshold.'

As soon as he heard this Khawaja Uthman in a mood of anger said, I will not be surprised if the man falls down from the upper storey and breaks his neck!'

After that he asked the spiritual disciple to return home. That disciple was still on his way home when he heard that the man had actually fallen and broken his neck. When he reached home he found the story was in fact a reality.

There is another case when on another occasion Khawaja Uthman Harooni helped a person who had no one to help him. It so happened that this man who came to him had lost his son and that son's whereabouts had not been known for a long time. It is but natural that the father could not bear long the separation from his son. He went to Khawaja Uthman and and submitted that he his son and that now he could no longer bear the separation; saying this he began to weep. Khawaja Uthman Harooni felt pity for the old man. He closed his eyes, meditated for a few minutes and then asked the man to go home. He gave him this word of comfort and cheer. 'You will find your son waiting for you at home'.

The man was a little diffident and doubtful of what Khawaja Uthman Harooni had said – but as soon as he reached home he found his son sitting there. The father embraced his son and brought him into the presence of Khawaja Uthman Harooni.

When the father and son were both sitting in the presence of Khawaja Uthman Harooni the father inquired from his son as to where he had been all that time. His son said that it so happened he was taken to a far off island where he was put in chains. His father asked, 'How did you come here?' He replied that a person (pointing to Khawaja Uthman Harooni) came there and broke his chains and freed him and then asked him to close his eyes. As soon as he closed his eyes he found himself at his own house.

He not only helped his spiritual disciples during their lifetime but there are instances where he helped them even after their death.

One of his spiritual disciples dies and his funeral was attended amongst others by Khawaja Uthman Harooni's caliph and sajjadanashin (spiritual successor) Khawaja Muinuddin Hasan Chishti. When the man had been buried people left but Khawaja Muinuddin stayed there.

All of a sudden he saw that the angels came there to torment the man. As soon as the angels came he also saw that his spiritual guide and teacher Khawaja Uthman Harooni appeared there with a stick in his hand and told the angels they should not put to torture the man as he was his disciple.

Thereupon the angels went and came again and said; 'It may be that he was your disciple but it was also true that he did not follow your teachings and precepts'. Thereupon Khawaja Uthman Harooni said that it was enough that he was a disciple. That affiliation counted a great deal, Upon this those angels who had come to give the dead body torture disappeared and other angels came and showered their blessings and gave and conferred peace upon the dead body.

Khawaja Uthman was very fond of *Sama*. By *Sama* is meant music. Among the Sufis *Sama* implies music concert. Music concert is what we call Qwaali. Qwaali is a little different from ordinary music or song. In Qwaali the theme is either the praise of the holy Prophet or of the saints. Sometimes verses are also recited that are based upon love and which convey some mystical connotation. Amongst the saints belonging to the Chishti order music is a fundamental plank (of spiritual practice); whereas in some orders, notably the Naqshbandi order, music is not in vogue.

Khawaja Uthman Harooni used to say that music is one of the secrets of God.

The Ulema in those days – by Ulema I mean the learned people – raised an objection as they thought music was anti-Islamic. They objected and there was a vehement opposition. It was so arranged that the Ulema would come and argue the matter with Khawaja Uthman Harooni. To this he agreed.

One day the Ulema came and Khawaja Uthman Harooni also attended the assembly of the learned people, the doctors of law. As soon as the Ulemas came before him they could not argue as they became speechless. They tried to speak but they could not do so. They tried to recollect their arguments but they were unable to. Then the Ulema, thinking it was due to Khawaja Uthman Harooni's spiritual powers, implored his forgiveness and as was his wont he gladly forgave them. As soon as he forgave them they regained their knowledge and their power of speech too was revived. He continued to hear Sama as he used to do and nobody thereafter raised any objection.

His Gospel Today

Modern people in modern times understand that standard of living implies that a man should lead an egotistic life entrenched in luxury, pomp, ostentation and display; whereas real standard of living implies beauty, grace and light.

Khawaja Uthman was an ambassador of goodwill and a poet of humanism and a staunch supporter of truth. He didn't distinguish between beauty and truth. To him truth was beauty and beauty was truth. The modern man, living in this age of crisis, living in this age of anxiety, living and being beset by many and multifarious difficulties and bearing all the stress of modern life, can and is capable of finding solace, peace, comfort and tranquillity – which are enshrined in his teachings and which point to a better way of life.

People run from post to pillar. They want more. They worship the glittering coin and they think that by money and by money alone they can find happiness. But happiness according to the Sufis and to the mystics is a thing which cannot be purchased in a market, not even in any market in the world. It is a strange thing which comes from within. It is a state of mind. It is the result of the harmonious working of the person and of his concentrating on things that really matter.

Contentment has always been the watchword of the Sufis. Contentment, to the Sufis is wealth, and it is wealth that is imperishable. A contented man is a happy man. Curtailment of desires leads to happiness; and the Sufis had shown that even in patched clothes, and even living under thatched roof, even living in mud walls, even being without clothes and other amenities furnished, they could not be sorry but they had the spirit of thankfulness. Now this spirit of thankfulness is also an important thing for spiritual progress and for spiritual growth. It is said that the man who does not offer thanks for the blessings given to him by God, they are taken away. This means it is a punishment for a man who does not offer thanks to God. To be thankful implies to be grateful and to be grateful implies that a man has the harmonious working and an insight into the actual possible realities of life. An ungrateful man is hated by society.

In all ages he has been hated, he has been condemned, he has been outlawed, he has been outcaste; but still there are so many black sheep who are not only insincere but ungrateful to man; and a man who is ungrateful to man must surely be ungrateful to God. It is laid down, and in very clear terms it has been laid down – you offer thanks and God says I will increase your blessings. Hazrat Khawaja Uthman Harooni had that spirit of thankfulness. He, for even an ordinary favour, for even an ordinary thing, would thank the one who had conferred an ostensible act upon him or before him. The difficulty of the modern age is that people assume double self and the Sufis and Khawaja Uthman Harooni both emphasise that sincerity is another virtue which should be tried. There are certain things that can be purchased in the market, but a Sufi, a mystic, a saint, goes out in search of those things which are not to be purchased by money – and now what are those things?

The question is what are those things? Those things are hope, belief, faith, patience, perseverance, contentment and optimism. These are very, very precious jewels. Without these things life is incomplete. Life will be a long tale of suffering and tribulations. The life of the man who does not purchase these traits is devoid of rhyme and rhythm. That man has no sense of proportion and no sense of perspective; and no way of adjusting himself to the modern world – leading him to a destination, which he does not know himself.

The toiling and tumbling masses and the so called affluent classes took Khawaja Uthman Harooni to be their preceptor and benefactor. He had deep sympathy for the common man. He believed that the lot of the common man was miserable indeed. Throughout his life he strenuously tried to elevate the conditions of those who were living in abject conditions of life. A man who gives a word of encouragement, a man who offers a priceless piece of advice, a man who advances some suggestion, indeed gives that which is of more value and of more worth than any title, estate, power or wealth.

Spiritual Genealogy

The Holy Prophet Muhammad (pbuh)

Hazrat Ali Murtaza bin Abi Talib, (ra)

Khawaja Hasan Basri, (ra)

Khawaja Abdul Wahid bin Zaid, (ra)

Khawaja Fazail bin Ayaz, (ra)

Khawaja Sultan Ibrahim bin Adhem, (ra)

Khawaja Sadeeduddin Marashee, (ra)

Khawaja Abi Hubera Basri, (ra)

Khawaja Mumshad Alu Denoori, (ra)

Khawaja Abu Ishaq Shami Chishti, (ra)

Khawaja Abu Ahmed Chishti, (ra)

Khawaja Abu Muhammad Chishti, (ra)

Khawaja Abu Yusuf Chishti, (ra)

Khawaja Moudoud Chishti, (ra)

Khawaja Hajji Sharif Zindani. (ra)

The Spread of His Message

Hazrat Khawaja Uthman Harooni had a very large following. Many came to him but few were chosen for the exalted office of caliph.

Beside Khawaja Muinuddin Hasan Chishti, who is his premier caliph and Sajjadanashin (spiritual successor), Hazrat Khawaja Fakhruddin Guidezi, Hazrat Sheikh Muhammad Turk Nar Nolvi, Qazi Qudwa, Sheikh Abdullah Qazi, Sheikh Safiuddin Ibrahim Razi, Shaikh Saadi Langochi and Sheikh Najinuddin Sughra had the honour and privilege of being his caliphs.

Among his murids (spiritual disciples) Hajji Rumi, Syed Muinuddin, Sultan II Tur Mish, Qazi Daniyal Qutri and Syed Arab occupy a prominent place.

In his own lifetime, as has been said, Khawaja Uthman appointed Khawaja Muinuddin Hasan Chishti as his spiritual successor. He entrusted to him all the holy relics which he had received from his spiritual guide Hazrat Hajji Sharif Zindani. Entrusting to him (Khawaja Muinuddin Hasan Chishti) the holy relics Khawaja Uthman Harooni emphatically said that he should be careful enough to keep these holy relics as he had kept them with him. After his passing away hi message was carried by, and his mission also received an impetus from Khawaja Muinuddin Hasan Chishti. His field of activity was mainly in the sub-continent of Indo-Pakistan and Bangladesh.

Khawaja Muinuddin Hasan Chishti passed a great portion of his life in this sub-continent. He preached the gospel of truth, spread the message and fulfilled the mission. During his own lifetime he appointed Hazrat Qutubuddin Bakhtiar Kaki as his Sajjadanashin or spiritual successor. Hazrat Qutubuddin lies buried in Mehrauli in New Delhi.

Hazrat Khawaja Qutubuddin Bakhtiar Kaki in his turn appointed Hazrat Baba Farid Masud Gange-i-Shakar as his Sajjadanashin. He lies buried in Pak Pattan in Pakistan.

Hazrat Baba Farid Masud Gange-i-Shakar appointed Khawaja Nizamuddin Aulia as his Sajjadanashin, whose tomb in new Destill an object of adoration to people. His 'urs or death anniversary is celebrated every year with great felicity and grandeur.

Baba Farid Masud Gange-i-Shakar had another eminent disciple and his name was Hazrat Alauddin Ali Ahmed Sabit of Kalyar. His tomb is in Kalyar. From these two disciples of Baba Farid Masud Gange-i-Shakar there arose two new scions of the order, I mean the Chishti Order, one was called Nizami and the other was called Sabiri: and thus the order grew.

Hazrat Nizamuddin Aulia during his own lifetime appointed Hazrat Nasiruddin Chirag of Delhi as his spiritual successor and Hazrat Alauddin Ali Ahmed appointed Hazrat Shemsuddin

Turk of Panipat as his spiritual successor. From these two persons the order grew in dimension.

The Nizami and the Sabiri orders were scions of the same Chishti Order. The order further grew and reached distant South India, Bengal and Gujerat. One of the eminent caliphs of Hazrat Nizamuddin Aulia, named Burhanuddin Gharib, went to the south and to the city of Burhanpur was named after him. Another caliph of Hazrat Nizamuddin Aulia, named Hazrat Siraj Akhi was a towering saint. Hazrat Mehboob Ilahi (beloved of God) – I mean Hazrat Nizamuddin Aulia, used to call him as the mirror of India. His caliph was a towering saint called Ala yl Haq. He did a lot of work in Bengal and he had a caliph known as Syed Ashraf Jehangir Samnani. He was a king of Samnan and he abdicated his throne and took to the path of Sufism. He came to India, became a murid (disciple) of Ala yl Haq. His tomb is in Kachocha.

Hazrat Syed Muhammad Gesoo Daraz who was a disciple of Hazrat Nasiruddin Chirag of Delhi, went to the south to preach and propagate the gospel of truth. His tomb at Gulbarga draws myriads of people – who go there to get his blessings.

The fatiha (prayer for the saint) of Hazrat Khawaja Uthman Harooni is conducted every month on the night of the fifth of the lunar month, in the Uthmani Gudri Shahi Khanqah at Ajmer. It is one of the important events obtaining in the Gudri Shahi Order of the Sufis.

Hazrat Khawaja Uthman Harooni had never been to Ajmer where his Sajjadanashin Khawaja Muinuddin Hasan Chishti lies buried, but a stately building stands as a tribute and as a reminder of his spiritual greatness. It so happened that when my uncle and spiritual guide of reverend memory – the late Hazrat Nawob Muhammad Khadim Shah Saheb, Zuberi Uthmani Moini Gudri Shah – better known as Nawob Saheb Gudri Shah Baba, went to Mecca to perform Hajj or pilgrimage a second time, he also paid his humble respects to the last resting place of Hazrat Khawaja Uthman Harooni. He was successful in obtaining some holy relics therefrom. The aforesaid holy relics are reverentially buried at the place which came to be known as Uthmani Chilla.

Poetry

Hazrat Khawaja Uthman Harooni was also a poet. His poetic nickname (Takhalus) was *Uthman*. Here is an English translation of one of his more famous verses in Persian.

I do not know why at last to have a longing look,

   I dance,

But I feel proud of the fondness that before the Friend,

   I dance,

Thou strikest the musical instrument and lo! Every time

   I dance!

In whatever way Thou causest me to dance, O Friend,

   I dance.

Come, O Beloved! See the spectacle that in the crowd,

of the intrepid and daring,

With a hundred ignominies, in the heart of the market,

I dance!

Blessed is recklessness that I trample underfoot the

very many acts of virtue.

Hail to piety! That with the robe and the turban,

I dance,

I am Uthman-i-Harooni and a friend of Sheikh Mansur,

They revile and rebuke, and on the gallows

I dance.

Conclusion

Hazrat Khawaja Uthman Harooni Chishti was in fact a candle. He was a lamp and he was a light too. He was a candle in the cottage of the poor. He was a lamp in the house of the rich, and he was a light everywhere in the circuitous path of life. Time and circumstance could not conspire to extinguish the Light.

Glossary

Alam al-jabarut*: the world of omnipotence; divine power.*

Alam al-lahut*: the world of divine being.*

Alam al-malakut*: the world of sovereignty – of dominion*

Bait ul Aqsa*: The Mosque at Jerusalem*

Baqa*: Abiding in Allah.*

Chilla: *the retreat of forty days.*

Fana:*th passing away of the attributes of self.*

Faqir*: A poor person in need of Allah.*

Faqr*: Poverty.*

Gudri: *the patched frock of a dervish.*

Hadi: *the guide, one of the qualities of Allah.*

Haqiqat: *The Reality.*

Ilm al-ladunni*.direct knowledge from on high which is the fruit of Iham (inspiration).*

Ilm-i-hikmat*: wisdom.*

Ilm-i-mjam: *spiritual state of gathering; comprehensiveness; unification.*

Jam' al-jam: *the state of gathering, in which the Sufi is so drowned in Allah that he does not see himself; unifying unification; the absorption of the all in Allah.*

Khirqat: *a patched garment.*

Kifayat: *abundance; sufficiency.*

Ma'rifat: *gnosis; cognition; wisdom.*

Ma'siyat: *sins, offences.*

Mumin; *a believer.*

Munkar: *name of the angel who, together with Nakir examines the soul of the deceased in the grave.*

Murshid: *spiritual guide.*

Nakir: *see above under Munkar.*

Namaz; *the ritual prayer (salat).*

Pir: *the spiritual guide.*

Pul Sirat: *the bridge over which the righteous will pass into paradise.*

Qaal: *discourses.*

Qalander: *a type of dervish.*

Qawwal: *professional singer at the Sama.*

Qiblat (Qibla): *the direction of Mecca for prayer*

Sahw: *sobriety*

Sajjada*: prayer carpet.*

Salik*: a traveller on the spiritual path.*

Saluk*: the travel; the wayfarer.*

Sama'*: The musical concert; to hear.*

Shariat*: exoteric revelation, religious laws*

Talwin*: change.*

Tariqat: *the Way, the Sufi path.*

Tawhid*: the unity of Allah.*

Ulema*: scholars of the religious sciences of Islam.*

Wafa: *fidelity.*

Zakat*: charity.*

Zulf*: a curling lock of hair.*

Brief Bibliography

Primary Sources:

Chishti, Muinuddin Hasan: Anis-al-Arwah; Lahore, 1928.

Diwan: Dhanbad; 1984.

Maktubat; (MS); Urdu translation; Lahore, nd.

Kash-al-Asrar (MS)

Hadith-al-Maarif (MS).

Risala Mawjudia (MS).

Afaq-o-Anfas (MS).

Ganj-al-Asrar (MS).

Kaki, Khawaja Qutubuddin Bhakhtyar.

Dalil-al-Arafin; Lahore; 1928.

Secondary Sources

Ahmad*, M.M. Zahruddin: Mystic Tendencies in Islam; Lahore; 1973.*

Ansari*, Muhammad Abdul Haq: Sufismand Shariah; Leicester; 1986.*

Arabi*, Ibn-al-: Journey to the Lord of power; The Hague; 1981.*

Arberry, *A. J.: An Introduction to the History of Sufism; Oxford; 1942. Sufism; London; 1950.Revelation and Reason in Islam; London 1957.*

Baldick, *Julian: Mystical islam; London; 1957.*

Brown, *John P.: The Dervishes. London; 1968.*

Burkhardt, *Titu: An Introduction to Sufi Doctrine; Lahore; 1973.*

Curry, *P.M.: The Shrine and Cult of Muin al-din Chishti of Ajmer; Delhi; 1989.*

Dehlavi, *Shaykh Abdul Haqq: Akhbar-al-Akhyar; Lahore; 1962.*

Eaton, *Richard Maxwell; Sufisof Bijapur; Princeton; 1978.*

Haeri, *Shaykh Fadhlalla: The Elements of Sufism; Longmead, Shaftsbury, Dorset; 1990.*

Hasan, *Khadim: Moin-al-Arwah; Ajmer; n.d.*

Hujwiri, *Ali bin Uthman al-:Kashf Al-Mahjub; Lahore; 1976.*

Jamali, *Hamid Bin Fazlullah: Sair-al-Arafin; Lahore; 1976.*

Jami, *Abdur-Rahman: Nafhat-al-Uns; (Urdu Translation); Lahore; n.d.*

Kalabadhi, *Abu Bakr al-:The Doctrine of the Sufis; Cambridge; 1979.*

Kirmani, Seyyed: *Muhammad Mubarak,Siyar-al-Aulia; Delhi; 1309. A.H.*

Lings*, Martin: What is Sufism?: London; 1975.*

Maneri*, Sharafuddin: The Hundred Letters; New York: 1980.*

Nasr*, Seyyed Hossein: Islamic Spirituality (2 vols); 1985 and 1991.*

Nicholson, *R.A.:The Mystics of Islam; London; 1963. The Idea of Personality in Sufism: Lahore; 1970. Studies in Islamic mysticism; Cambridge; 1978.*

Rizvi*, Saiyid Athar abbas: A History of Sufism in India (2 vols); New Delhi; 1978 and 1983.*

Sharib, *Zahurul Hasan; Khawaja Gharib Nawaz; Lahore; 1990.Biographies and Sayings of the Chishti Saint; Ajmer; 1981.The Mystic Philosophy of Khawaja Moinuddin Hasan Chishti; Ajmer; 1980. The Life and Teachings of Khawaja Moinuddin Hasan Chishti; Ajmer; 1990.The Sufi saints and Shrines of Indo-Pakistan and Bangladesh; New Delhi; n.d. Live, the Message of Khawaja Uthman Harooni; Southampton; 1981.The Psalm of Life: Southampton; 1990. The Psalm of Love: Southampton; 1990. The Psalm of Light;: Southampton; 1990. Abu Said Abi'l Khair and his Rubaiyat; Southampton; 1993.Hafiz and his Rubaiyat; Southampton; 1990.Sarmad and his Rubaiyat; Southampton; 1994. Moin-al-Hind; Delhi; 1988.Naib-i-Rasul fil Hind; Agra; 1982. Dilli ke Bais Khawaja: Delhi; 1988. Dastaney Khawaja: Agra; n.d. Khum Khana-i-Tasawuf: Delhi; 1987.Nazi-e-Khawaja Fakhruddin Abul Abil Khair; Delhi; 1994.Shaikh Kabir BabaFarid uddin Ganj-e-Shakar; Delhi; 1994. Khawaja*

Moinuddin Chishti; Den Haag; 1993.De Roos van Bagdad; Den Haag; 1993.The Path of Positive Living: Suggerimenti per una Vita Poisitiva; Trieste and Southampton; 1993.The Culture of the Sufis; Southampton; 1999.

Shah, *Idries the sufis; London; 1984.*

Shah, *Sirdar Iqbal Ali; Islamic Sufism; Lahore; 1993.*

Skali, *Faouzi; La Voi Soufie; Paris; 1985.*

Subhan, *J.A.: Sufism: its Saints and Shrines; Lucknow; 1960.*

Suhrewardi, *Shihabuddin Abu Hafs:'Umar; Awarif-al-Ma'arif (Urdu translation); Lahore; 1977.*

Sulami, *Muhammad ibn al-Husayn al-: The Book of Sufi Chivalry; The Hague, 1983.*

Trimmingham, *J. Spencer: The Sufi Orders in Islam; Oxford; 1971.*

Troll, *Christian W.: Muslim Shrines in India; Delhi; 1989.*

Valiuddin, *Dr Mir: Contemplative Disciplines in Sufism; The Hague; 1980. The Qur'anic Sufism; Lahore; 1978.*

www.ingramcontent.com/pod-product-compliance
Lightning Source LLC
Chambersburg PA
CBHW031403040426
42444CB00005B/402